Res

THE ROMANCE
OF
MADAME TUSSAUD'S

By

John Theodore Tussaud

Died Oct 13 1943.

grandson of Madame Tussaud

Reserve Stock

London - ODHAMS LIMITED
39 King Street, Covent Garden, W.C. 2

1920

CONTENTS

I

CONTENTS 3

CONTENTS

LIST OF ILLUSTRATIONS

5

PREFACE

THE earliest information we have concerning
Madame Tussaud is that she was born in Switzer-
land on the 7th of December, 1760, and was the
only child of Joseph and Marie Grosholtz. Her
mother was the daughter of a Swiss clergyman.

She married on the 20th of October, 1795, François
Tussaud, who, it appears, was her junior by seven
years. We are able to trace his family back as
far as 1630, when his great-great-grandfather, one
Denis Tusseaud—for that is how he spelt his name
—was born.

There is documentary evidence that Denis was
brought from Burgy to Mâcon in 1631, his family
also coming from Burzy, close by, in 1658.

His descendants lived at Mâcon for more than
a century, their occupation being generally that
of workers in metal.

The great-grandfather of François was Henry
Tusseaud (1684–1717), and his grandfather's name
was Claude (1716–1767).

François' father (1744–1786) was the first
of the family to adopt the present spelling of
the name, although we find that various
members of the family used the forms Tussot,
Tusseau, Tuissiaud, Tussiaut, Tusseaut, Tussiau,
or Thusseaud.

Madame Tussaud's marriage does not appear
to have been a happy one, for we learn that in
1800—two years before she came to England—
she separated from her husband, of whom we
hear nothing further, although he is known to

have been living in Paris in the lifetime of his grandsons.

The foundress of the famous Exhibition had two sons, Joseph and Francis. Francis (1800–1873) had several sons, the eldest of whom, Joseph Randall (1831–1892), who was a student and exhibitor at the Royal Academy, was the father of the author of this book.

Mr. John Theodore Tussaud was born in Kensington on the 2nd of May, 1858, and at the age of six was sent to St. Charles's College, London, where he came under the influence of Cardinal Manning, who took a keen personal interest in his welfare.

Some six years later he was transferred to Ramsgate, where he benefited by the training he received from the Benedictine monks at St. Augustine's.

In the year 1889 he married Ruth Helena, daughter of Thomas Grew. There are seven sons and three daughters of the marriage.

Mr. Tussaud, like his father, has exhibited at the Royal Academy. His occasional contributions to literature have been welcomed by thoughtful readers, and he is a recognised authority on historical matters relating to the French Revolution and the First Empire.

Seventeen great-grandsons of Madame Tussaud took an active part in the war, all, without exception, serving in the British Army. Two were killed and most of the others wounded.

WILLIAM E. HURT.

MIDDLE TEMPLE,
     1st November, 1919.

JOHN THEODORE TUSSAUD.

[To face p. 9.

THE ROMANCE
OF
MADAME TUSSAUD'S

CHAPTER I

Mr. Tussaud first enters his father's studio—Reverie—Madame
Tussaud's uncle forsakes the medical profession for art—
Madame's birth and parentage—A Prince's promise.

IT was at the age of fourteen and in the year 1872
that I first entered my father's studio, and well
I remember the bright summer morning I passed
its threshold to place myself under his tuition.

It was an odd rememorative sort of place, the
eeriness of which sat uneasily on the mind of, I fear,
a somewhat jocose and irresponsible youth.

The surroundings somehow seemed to force
upon my mind the memories of men and things I
must have heard about or dreamt of, or with
whom I had been in some way made familiar.
Moreover, the place was so out of touch with the
ordinary affairs of life, so reposeful and secluded
amid th din and turmoil of the world outside.

The studio stood well in the rear of an old-world
residence, known as Salisbury House, in the parish
of Marylebone. Here the family had long lived.

9

The house confronted what, in my early days, was then still designated the New Road. Upon its site there has been since erected the imposing classic palace designed to accommodate the hitherto poorly housed Corporation of the borough.

Whenever I recall this eventful day there readily springs to my mind the circumstance that I found my father busily engaged in modelling a new portrait of the Prince of Wales—the late King Edward—for whose recovery from a very dangerous illness the nation had recently held a Day of Thanksgiving.

From this day onward I may claim to have acted as something more than a mere spectator of that long procession of models wrought by my father's diligent hands. Each one necessitated the making of some small sketch, some character-istic study, that has helped to swell as strange a collection of memorials as ever existed of men and events of bygone days.

It is amid these surroundings that I now sit to begin the writing of these chapters ; and a strangely engrossing retrospect they reveal. Five genera-tions of my family have contributed towards them, and now, on a modelling stool by my side, there stands the promising work of a son who will, I trust, one day follow me to carry on the work.

During the quietude of those hours that succeed the labours of the day, and when the last studio hand has closed the door behind him, I take the opportunity of penning this brief history. Often in the moving shadows of the twilight or in the flickering flame of a falling ember I fancy I see life and movement in the faces that gaze down upon me, quickened, as it were, to respond to the memories their features evoke.

But for me, at least, there is little that is disquieting in their scrutiny. For the most part they are old familiars, and a long acquaintance has set us wonderfully at our ease.

As the eye passes from the semblance of one celebrity to that of another, how vividly they carry one's thoughts back through King Edward's reign, the long years Queen Victoria sat upon the throne, the days of William IV., the reign and regency of " The First Gentleman of Europe," and far back into the days of good " Farmer George " !

Even though set among the strong and characteristic features of the leading men of these memorable reigns, the striking countenance of Napoleon can be discerned without hesitation, and his familiar features force me in imagination to undergo the ordeal of crossing the Channel to retrace the course this narrative takes and discover my ancestress under the domination of the First Consul, then pushing in hot haste his fortune at the point of the bayonet, and fast traversing the hazardous road leading to the throne of France.

Somehow we do not find this long and curious retrospect illumined by any very strong ray of human happiness. Even the overshadowing head and shoulders of the great Napoleon do not conceal from our vision the dismal heads of the revolutionists ; indeed, if they had been hidden from our sight, could these ghoulish impressions ever be effaced from our memory? And so, behind Bonaparte, one's eyes sight the sinister heads of Robespierre, Fouquier-Tinville, Carrier, Hébert— merciless creatures who gambled with the lives of their fellow men for high positions, and multiplied these awful human stakes that they might hold themselves secure.

There, too, in the falling light, one perceives the faces of Louis XVI. and his Queen, Marie Antoinette, the two most notable and pitiful victims of the Reign of Terror—a reign, forsooth, in which these ill-starred sovereigns, the descendants of generations of kings, were but the poorest and saddest of subjects.

The vista is long and hazy, but it is not too dim for one to observe upon a bracket the visage of the great Voltaire, with its leering eyes and sardonic grin. His bust is *vis-à-vis* with the ponderous head of the idealist Rousseau, with its heavy forehead and its short, narrow chin.

And so face after face peers down upon me, carrying the mind back with unfailing steps until is reached the true source from which this dramatic story springs.

.   .   .   .

In the year 1758, so far afield as the city of Berne, a certain young Swiss, named Christopher Curtius, was earnestly employing his days as a medical practitioner.

With the object of improving himself in his profession he had taken to modelling the limbs and organs of the human body in wax. He soon extended the scope of his labours to the execution of many miniature portraits in that same plastic material, and gained the patronage of many of the leading members of the aristocracy. In this work he succeeded well, and towards his latter days in Berne he practised rather as an artist than as a family doctor.

It is as the maternal uncle of Madame Tussaud, the subject of these memoirs, that Christopher Curtius comes under our consideration.

Madame Tussaud was the child of one Joseph Grosholtz, who lost his life when serving on the Staff of General Wurmser during the Seven Years' War, a couple of months or so before she was born. He was of purely Swiss parentage, and the family to this day prides itself on being of Burgundian Swiss stock.

Although Marie Grosholtz was not married until the year 1795, it will be well to refer to her henceforth as Madame Tussaud, under which name she is universally known.

Madame Grosholtz and her child seem to have been the only relatives possessed by Curtius, who

B

later induced his sister to take up her residence
with him, doubtless with the object of taking
control of the affairs of his household.

It was when Curtius had fully established himself
as an artist in Berne that an incident took place,
about the year 1762, which led to important
consequences.

The Prince de Conti had been losing favour at
the Court of his royal cousin, Louis XV., a
circumstance mainly due, we are told, to the
Prince's excessive popularity with the Army and
a certain independent bearing he adopted towards
the King and his favourites. The King's mistress,
Madame de Pompadour, did not hesitate to show
her resentment at de Conti's lack of deference.

According to all accounts, the Prince did not take
his position very much to heart, for, in truth, an
estrangement between the Court and the representatives of his house afforded little in the nature of a
new experience. At any rate, he shook the dust
of the capital off his boots, and set out on a tour
through Europe.

On this journey he tarried for some days in the
city of Berne, betraying a keen desire to participate
in all that mediæval town could afford him by way
of interest and entertainment.

Among these Curtius's studio—which had now
acquired something of the dignity of a private
museum—was not allowed to escape his attention.
No account of his visit to this establishment has

been handed down, but a few words uttered by the Prince on leaving conveyed, beyond all doubt, his genuine admiration for the doctor-artist's skill in his new profession as a sculptor in wax.

" If you will leave Berne and come to Paris, I will undertake to find you a suitable atelier in which to carry on your work, and hold myself responsible for your receiving as many commissions as you feel disposed to execute. Come," he urged. " You will not regret it."

One wonders what kindred foibles, what curious traits of disposition in common, existed between this Prince and the artist that there should have been struck so readily a chord of sympathy between them. For the offer, as we shall hereafter learn, had not been lightly made, nor had its ready acceptance been inspired without betraying a ready confidence most men would have deemed it highly imprudent to concede.

CHAPTER II

IN response to the Prince de Conti's invitation, Curtius left Berne for Paris a few months later, and for once the time-honoured adage proffering a warning to those prone to rely upon the promises of princes had no bearing, for this Prince kept his word.

On his arrival at Paris, Curtius found a handsome suite of apartments awaiting him at the Hôtel d'Aligre, hard by the Croix du Trahoir in the Rue St. Honoré. They were spacious and well furnished, and in style and comfort far exceeded his expectation. The Rue St. Honoré on the north, the Rue Bailleul on the south, the Rue de l'Arbre Sec on the east, and the Rue des Poulies on the west, outline to this day the ground on which the hotel, with its gardens, then stood.

The Hôtel d'Aligre was a place that had seen better days. It had, like so many of the great family dwellings that existed in Paris towards the end of the eighteenth century, demanded of

CHRISTOPHER CURTIUS.

(A Portrait Study by John T. Tussaud)

[To face p. 16.

its owners a longer and more speedily replenished purse than they possessed. The sheltering of a stately and magnificent household had long been unknown to this once famous residence, and its handsome rooms had been divided up and let as separate tenements.

The building contained a fine *salon*, which at one time was placed by a Chancellor d'Aligre at the service of the Grand Council, and so late as the year of Curtius's arrival in Paris we hear of it being used for an exhibition of pictures displayed under the ægis of the Académie de Saint Luc. Of this académie Curtius was soon elected a member, and it may be presumed that some of his own works were shown in the exhibition.

During its latter days the hotel figured under a dual appellation, the ancient name of d'Aligre being prefaced by that of the renowned Schomberg. Finally it was known to the good citizens of Paris, shortly before its total disappearance, as the Old Hôtel Schomberg d'Aligre.

This building occupied a position that could hardly have been better chosen for Curtius's purpose, for it stood in the very heart and throng of the busy capital—that is to say, close to the Louvre and at no great distance from the Tuileries —and was surrounded by the houses of the wealthiest and most influential inhabitants of the city.

We should like to follow the footsteps of Curtius, and enter with him into his new home in Paris ;

C

but with the meagre information we have concerning these early days in his career we can only picture him as settling down to his work and drawing around him many famous patrons, to some of whom we shall have to refer as we make progress with our story.

Doubtless the ideals he had conceived of the French capital as a citizen in far-off Berne would not have squared with the actual state in which he found the city when he took up his domicile within it.

Report had carried the splendours of Versailles far beyond the frontiers of France, and might well have enlivened the imagination of an artist like Curtius, who, doubtless, would have hoped to enjoy the pleasure of witnessing them for himself; but on his arrival in the capital he found the glories of the palaces had set, and that the Court of Louis XV. had not only grown dull, but had even gone out of fashion.

The King himself had become weary of the great Court functions and sumptuous entertainments, and now preferred to indulge in complete seclusion the appetites that still remained to him. The military exploits of his reign had not brought him any great renown, and in recent years he had suffered reverses that had cast a gloom over these closing days of his life.

He had also been reminded more than once that the levelling hand of Death took no heed of rank and power. That dread visitor had already unceremoniously claimed the King's son (the Dauphin) and his wife, and his own neglected Queen, Marie Leczinska, was fast failing in health.

The temper of the people towards the King had undergone a great change, and the days of " Well-Beloved "-ness had long since departed. During the reign of his predecessor, Louis XIV., the excessive taxation and the state of semi-serfdom had been borne by the lower classes with something like resignation, for they had received some compensation through the glory of his military achievements and the extension of his power. But small reason had they for so patiently bearing the ever-increasing burdens that had signalised the reign of his successor, Louis XV., whose military exploits had brought the country little by way of glory, and whose career had naught to show but a long life of wanton extravagance, combined with a painful disregard for the welfare of his people.

What Curtius did in the four years that succeeded his arrival in Paris one cannot say for certain ; but there is little doubt that he was busily engaged in executing commissions for his numerous and ever-increasing patrons, whose liberality and kindness not only equalled, but far surpassed, the Prince de Conti's promises.

It is quite evident that soon after his arrival Curtius tried his deft hands upon a model of the Queen of Louis XV., and it is this comparatively early work that constitutes one piece among a mere half-dozen examples that have been handed down to us. Probably the influence of his friend, the Prince de Conti, aided him in obtaining this commission.

It was after having practised his profession as artist for some years that Curtius repaired to Berne for the purpose of fetching his sister and her little daughter.

That was in the year 1766, and Madame Tussaud was then about six years old. On the authority of her *Memoirs*, published in 1838, it would appear that she was born at Berne in the year 1760 ; but documentary evidence exists which appears to indicate that her birth actually took place a year later. Be that as it may, we first hear of her when she accompanied her mother to Paris as the guest of her uncle.

This brief review will not permit us to dwell long on the early days of the young girl in Paris, nor on those events that prefaced the outbreak of the Revolution. Truth to say, between 1766 and 1789—a matter of twenty-three years—the details concerning the lives of Curtius and his niece are neither very full nor very clearly defined. This seems to be all of a piece with the nature of the work they produced, for it is astonishing, having regard to the considerable output, how small a quantity of it has been handed down to us.

LOUIS XVI. AND THE DUKE OF ORLÉANS.

(*Specimens of the few existing examples of Curtius's miniature work. Modelled from life shortly before the outbreak of the French Revolution*).

[To face p. 21

One has, therefore, little material to assist him in gaining an insight into the artists' careers, or to guide in the forming of a just opinion either as to the exact character of their work or the nature of their subjects. Miniatures in coloured wax, modelled in fairly high relief and framed and glazed in the ordinary way as pictures, seem to offer a general idea and the best conception of the work that emanated from the studio during these momentous years, so pregnant with meaning for the near future.

The pity of the loss is that the work, taken direct from life, afforded a faithful record of important personages. Of this there is ample proof, and that the models should have been of so ephemeral a character is a matter of great regret, extending far beyond the feelings of the artists' descendants. Yet, when one remembers the hatred of the populace towards the aristocrats and those holding authority under the Old Régime, it is not to be wondered at that many portraits should have shared, with their originals, the destructive effects of the antipathy that was shown both to patrons of art and to the art itself. It goes without saying that during the Reign of Terror people would be disposed to hide, or even to destroy, any art subject in their possession indicating their attachment to the Royalists.

CHAPTER III

A GOOD deal of hearsay and some incontestable
evidence helps to fill the hiatus between the time
Curtius came to Paris and the outbreak of the
Revolution.

Although the many years spent by Curtius in
the production of miniatures in coloured wax do
not appear to have brought him a very great or a
very wide reputation, yet they were the means of
leading him to the modelling of life-size portraits
of this same material, with the express intention
in forming them into a collection solely for the
object of exhibiting them to the public.

Now it is to this important departure in the
treatment of his works that we owe the present
Madame Tussaud's Exhibition, an establishment with which his name must be for ever
associated.

He seems to have set his mind upon this venture
round about the year 1776, and some years later
to have opened a Museum of life-size portrait

BENJAMIN FRANKLIN.
(*Modelled from life, in Paris, by Christopher Curtius for his Exhibition*)

[To face p. 23.

models at the Palais Royal, an enterprise that was soon to be followed by the opening of a second Exhibition of a far more renowned and interesting character on the Boulevard du Temple, to which we shall have occasion to refer more than once.

The Museum at the Palais Royal seems to have proved a lucrative concern, and to have been devoted to the portraits of men and women of position, holding for the time being a prominent place in the public eye. Little is known concerning it, except for a few meagre and commonplace references in the literature of the period, and it may, to all intents and purposes, be considered as relegated to the domain of the forgotten past.

We shall not, however, find ourselves able to dispose of the Exhibition on the Boulevard du Temple without rendering an account of it, for in the course of a few years it figured very largely in the Revolution, and had associated with it several incidents of an important and far-reaching character.

There is the record about this time of an acquaintance between the sculptor and Benjamin Franklin, the American statesman and philosopher.

Franklin had come to Paris in December, 1776, " to transact the business of his country at the Court of France," his chief purpose being to obtain political and financial assistance in consolidating the newly formed United States of America.

Curtius and his niece—now a young woman of sixteen years—had the pleasure of entertaining the Doctor, who took considerable interest in their work. Not only did he commission them to execute several distinct portraits of himself, but he also ordered models of many other notable characters of the day. One of his own portraits is the identical figure which has been shown at Madame Tussaud's ever since.

This model was executed in 1783, in which year Franklin assumed great prominence as one of the signatories to the Treaty of Peace between the Mother Country and the United States, which recognised the latter as an independent nation. The figure in question is a life-size one ; but, in addition to this, Curtius, aided by his capable niece, who was now earnestly supporting her uncle in his work, produced several miniature portraits of the statesman which went directly into his possession. Indeed, it is well known that Franklin had in his rooms in Paris many works that had emanated from Curtius's studio.

In Franklin's *Autobiography* there is an account of his home in Market Street, Philadelphia, in which he finally settled, and the following extract under the date 13th July, 1787, from a journal kept by an old friend of his, the Reverend Dr. Manasseh Cutler, a distinguished scholar and botanist, of Hamilton, Massachusetts, who had

THREE VIEWS OF VOLTAIRE'S HEAD.
Modelled from life by Christopher Curtius.

(This work was executed in Paris during the spring of 1778, a few weeks before Voltaire's death)

[T. face p. 25.]

recently paid him a visit, shows that he took with him from Paris a number of miniatures, many of which he had obtained from Curtius :

> Over his mantel he has a prodigious number of medals, busts and casts in wax or plaster of paris, which are the effigies of the most noted characters in Europe.

When Franklin returned to America in 1785 there sailed with him, on board the same ship, Houdon, the eminent French sculptor, who had been in his early student days a friend and companion of Curtius, who engaged his services, and to whom he rendered considerable assistance in his work.

Houdon's skill was highly appreciated by Franklin, and the object of the journey to America was that the sculptor might execute a statue of Washington for the State of Virginia, the instructions for the work coming from both Franklin and Jefferson. The voyage was made in the *London Packet*, and the date of the embarkation was the 27th of July, 1785.

Perhaps the most famous man of this period was the satirist, philosopher, and dramatist, Voltaire, who, throughout the whole of his long life, had championed the cause of the people against arbitrary and despotic power.

After an absence of twenty-eight years the aged Voltaire left his home on the shores of Geneva and returned to Paris, arriving there on the 10th of February, 1778. He was welcomed by an ovation that might well have befitted the home-coming of a great conqueror.

Curtius's reputation at that time stood at its highest, and Voltaire gave him several sittings soon after his arrival. It is owing to this circumstance that the artist was able to place among the models of his recently opened Exhibition on the Boulevard du Temple a life-size standing figure of this popular idol.

It is a matter of exceptional interest that the selfsame figure still exists, and is shown to-day as one of the most attractive and notable objects in Madame Tussaud's, where it has stood for just upon a century and a half.

Besides producing this figure, Curtius took the opportunity the sittings afforded him of executing several miniature models, one of them representing the philosopher during his last moments. To this he gave the title of "The Dying Socrates." Several copies of this are known to exist, and we give an illustration of the one in the Tussaud collection. These were the last portraits produced of him from life, and they were completed none too soon.

The stirring reception accorded Voltaire on his arrival in Paris, to which he responded with great energy, coupled with the strenuous effort and anxiety attending his personal superintendence

"THE DYING SOCRATES."
Portrait of Voltaire at the time of his death.
(*Wax miniature modelled by Christopher Curtius*)

of his new tragedy, *Irene*, soon affected his
health. The sittings were given during the months
of March and April, and on the following 30th of
May his eventful life terminated at the age of
eighty-four.

CHAPTER IV

IN the year 1780 the ill-fated Louis XVI. had been
six years on the throne, and Curtius by this time
had become well ingratiated with the followers
of the New Régime.

Among the many distinguished visitors who
honoured Curtius's studio with their presence
in 1780 was one who was destined to exercise
a great influence on Madame Tussaud's life. This
was the King's sister, Madame Elizabeth of France,
who, at the time we speak of, was sixteen years
of age. Her disposition was singularly sweet
and charming, and the keen interest she took in
the models and mysteries of the studio caused her
to bestow upon the niece of Curtius very special
attention.

Madame Elizabeth, according to her young
protégée, was of medium height and slight build,
her forehead was high and intellectual, and she
had kind, soft, blue eyes. Her expression and

28

MADAME ELIZABETH OF FRANCE.
Sister of Louis XVI. and Patroness of Madame Tussaud.

(A Portrait Study by John T. Tussaud)

[To face p. 28.

demeanour were most sympathetic, and on the slightest provocation her amiable countenance became wreathed in smiles, the parting lips revealing a perfect set of teeth.

So infatuated did Madame Elizabeth become with this pleasant work of modelling in coloured wax, which was soon to become a veritable craze, that she asked Madame Tussaud to instruct her in the art, and for that purpose invited her to live with her in her apartments at the Palace of Versailles, for the Princess seldom visited Paris.

Her overtures to his niece met with little opposition on the part of Curtius, who, in spite of the fact that he had decided leanings towards the cause of the people, yet, in order to further his relative's interests, readily gave his permission to her accompanying the Princess. This concession Curtius must have made at some sacrifice, for it deprived him of his niece's society and of the help she was then rendering him in his studio.

Madame Tussaud accordingly bade her uncle farewell, and left Paris for Versailles.

The quarters then occupied by Madame Elizabeth were situated at the end of the façade of the south wing of the palace, and looked out upon the Swiss Lake.

One wonders whether the fascinating work of modelling in wax was the sole influence that prompted Madame Elizabeth's friendly feeling towards Madame Tussaud. The Princess had already shown a marked predilection for the Swiss, for both at the palace and on her own private estate of Montreuil hard by she had many Swiss people about her.

Unfortunately, little is known of the life of Madame Tussaud either at Versailles or at Montreuil, which the King presented to his sister with the understanding that she should continue to make Versailles her official home until she attained the age of twenty-four.

We are told that the Princess was very fond of modelling sacred subjects, and many of these works produced by her own hands she gave away to her friends. She showed her attachment to Madame Tussaud in many ways, and required her to sleep in an adjoining apartment.

Curtius's niece often found herself engaged in many duties besides those associated with modelling in wax, and it was no unusual thing for the girl to be made the means of conveying alms to the Princess's numerous pensioners.

For nine years she enjoyed the confidence and almost daily company of her patroness, and throughout the long life vouchsafed to her she deemed them the happiest she had known. Seldom could she be brought to dwell upon these days, or call to mind the fate of her illustrious pupil and the other members of the Royal Family she then so often encountered, without the tears, sooner or later, welling to her eyes. Indeed, not even after the

MADAME TUSSAUD
at the age of 20.
(*A Portrait Study by John T. Tussaud*)

[To face p. 30.

passage of some sixty years, when her own days were drawing to a close, and when one might have expected her grief to have become assuaged, could she restrain her emotion at the memory of their sad and tragic end.

We have already referred to the second and larger Exhibition opened by Curtius on the Boulevard du Temple. A collection of wax figures representing famous personages, living and dead, attired in their everyday costume, and exhibiting their usual pose and attitude, was known as a " Cabinet de Cire."

The house wherein Curtius opened this second Exhibition was formerly occupied by Foulon, the Minister of Finance, who earned public execration by his ill-timed suggestion that if the people could not get sufficient bread they might eat hay. When the Revolution broke out Foulon was one of the first victims for the mob to vent its rage upon. They hanged him, decapitated the body, and then paraded the streets with his head stuck on a pike, between his lips being placed a wisp of hay in memory of the cruel sneer at the people's want.

For his Exhibition Curtius modelled several notable groups. Three of these call for some mention.

The first was a representation of the Royal Family dining in public, a curious ceremonial of that period. There was, within the walls of the Palace of Versailles, a chapel whither the family repaired to hear mass every morning; and on Sundays, after returning from prayer, they held a grand *couvert* in the palace. The dining-table was in the form of a horseshoe, the *Cent Suisse* (or Swiss Bodyguard) formed a circle around it, and, between them, the spectators were permitted to view the august party at their dinner.

To this spectacle everyone had access, provided the gentlemen were fully dressed—that is, had a bag-wig, sword, and silk stockings—and the ladies were correspondingly attired. Even if their clothes were threadbare the visitors were not turned back; nor were they admitted, however well clad, unless they presented themselves as etiquette prescribed.

The costume of the Swiss Bodyguard was magnificent, being similar to that worn by Henry IV. of France. It comprised a hat with three white feathers, short robe, red pantaloons or long stockings (all in one, and slashed at the top with white silk), black shoes with buckles, sash, sword, and halbert.

The Royal Family generally remained three-quarters of an hour at table. The spectacle was such an interesting one that Curtius, ever alive, as his successors have been, to satisfy the popular imagination, modelled a group for his Exhibition depicting the incident.

The second tableau represented an Indian group. In the grounds of the Palace of Versailles

are two residences, the Grand Trianon and the
Petit Trianon, the latter having been a favourite
retreat of Marie Antoinette because of its secluded
position and charming attractions.

Curtius—assisted by his niece, who was now a
full-grown woman, sensible of her responsibilities,
and able to execute commissions of her own—
modelled a group of figures, consisting of the envoys
of Tippoo Sahib and several sepoys in their
picturesque Eastern costumes, which was arranged
under a tent placed in the Grand Trianon.

Tippoo Sahib was the Sultan of Mysore, and he
had sent to Louis XVI. to invoke his assistance in
expelling the British from his dominions.

On the 10th of August, 1788, after spending
the night at the Grand Trianon, the envoys were
escorted to the Palace of Versailles, and received
with great pomp.

This was one of the last occasions on which
Madame Elizabeth appeared in public at the
palace and on which the King was able to receive
freely the representatives of a foreign Power.
The winter that followed was long and severe,
and had much to do with hastening the outbreak
of the Revolution and the downfall of the monarchy.

We do not know for certain whether the commission for the third group was prompted by
Madame Elizabeth or by Marie Antoinette herself,
but we know for certain that it was one of the
groups shown in the Petit Trianon before those

D

disturbing elements manifested themselves that heralded the terrible upheaval which was to come. The tableau comprised the seated figures of Louis XVI. and Marie Antoinette with their young children, the Dauphin and the Duchesse d'Angoulême, all attired in full Court costume.

A very special interest attaches to this group, inasmuch that, except for the renovation necessitated by the long passage of time, it is now shown within the walls of the present Exhibition exactly as it was when first modelled.

While Madame Tussaud was fully occupied at Versailles her uncle was busy with his Museum in Paris.

In 1783 Curtius added to his collection on the Boulevard du Temple the " Caverne des Grands Voleurs," which we may fairly regard as the forerunner of the present Chamber of Horrors.

There seems to be some doubt as to the distinctive character of Curtius's two Exhibitions. One authority informs us that his rooms at the Palais Royal contained the effigies of famous and celebrated men, and that the venture on the Boulevard du Temple was devoted to those of notorious and infamous scoundrels. One cannot say for certain what were the characteristics of the two collections at this time, but there can be no doubt that both attracted great numbers of people for a very long period.

The descriptive accounts of Parisian amusements

MARIE ANTOINETTE, THE DAUPHIN, AND THE
DUCHESSE D'ANGOULÊME.

(*Models taken from life and exhibited for some time in Le Petit Trianon
at Versailles*)

[To face p. 34.

of the time make mention of Curtius's " Cabinet
de Cire "—or, to make use of the titles given to it
on a copperplate etching of that period by Martial,
" Théatre des Figures de Cire, ou Théatre Curtius "
—as a sight well worthy of inviting the attention
of persons of rank and condition. " One may see,"
said Dulaure in 1791, " waxen coloured figures of
celebrated characters in all stations of life."

Upon closing the Exhibition at the Palais Royal,
Curtius conveyed its figures to the Boulevard du
Temple, wherein merged all the models that had
been previously on view, thus combining the peculiar
characteristics of the two establishments and
constituting the Madame Tussaud's Exhibition as
we know it to-day.

CHAPTER V

WE are now approaching the day when the long-pent-up storm, threatening for so great a while, was about to burst, and we must contemplate King Louis XVI. and his advisers seeking for a means to placate a people at last stirred to resentment through the cruel and unjust burdens it had for generations been made to bear.

The murmurings which had long been general and indefinite were now resolving themselves into a hatred fast becoming focused upon the rich and the powerful, many of whom, it must be added, were also arrogant and dissolute.

A rude awakening among some of these, who had at last been brought to realise the imminence of the convulsion, induced them to advocate with much haste and little discretion certain concessions. These were obviously granted as acts of expediency, and with as little derogation as possible from their own interest, rather than out of any sympathy for a distressed and desperate people clamouring for relief.

So, early in 1789, the King was prompted to resort to an expedient which had not been adopted since the year 1614. He summoned the States-General to meet together at Versailles on the 5th of May, 1789.

In the deliberations of this National Council the King and his Ministers looked for support and guidance to meet the difficulties that beset them. But matters took an unexpected course. The Deputies of the Third Estate, which outnumbered the First and Second put together, demanded that all three Estates should sit and vote as one whole indissoluble body. In spite of opposition they pushed their demand to a successful issue, and, grasping control of both legislative and executive power, forthwith resolved themselves into a permanent constitutional assembly.

The King soon found himself confronted by an irresistible authority, including a majority of men who betrayed little concern for his prerogative, and manifested a strong sympathy with the cause of the people.

In such stirring times as those which were now being experienced in France, Curtius turned to the advocates of the people's cause for many of his subjects for his new Exhibition. Among these were many who were to figure largely in the Revolution.

Special mention must be made of two figures, added about this date, namely, Necker and Philippe,

Duke of Orléans, for their models had an important bearing upon the events that followed.

Necker, at the time his model was made by Curtius and Madame Tussaud, was the French Minister of Finance. In 1775 he had claimed for the State the right of fixing the price of grain and, if necessary, of prohibiting exportation ; a year later he was made Director of the Treasury, and in 1777 he became Director-General of Finance.

His retrenchments were bitterly opposed by Queen Marie Antoinette; and his famous *Compte Rendu*, in 1781, occasioned his dismissal at that time. Some of his measures, such as his adjustment of taxes and his establishment of State-guaranteed annuities and State pawnshops, were a boon to suffering France. He retired to Geneva, but in 1787 returned to Paris, and, when M. de Calonne cast doubt on the *Compte Rendu*, he published a justification which drew upon him his banishment from Paris.

Recalled to office in September, 1788, he quickly made himself a popular hero by recommending the summoning of the States-General, to which reference has already been made.

On the 11th of July, 1789, he received the royal command to leave France at once ; but the fall of the Bastille, three days later, frightened the King into recalling him, amid the wildest popular enthusiasm.

The Duke of Orléans, the famous Egalité, was

another hero of the people at this time. He was looked upon coldly at Court owing to his dissolute habits.

London was frequently visited by him, and he became an intimate friend of the Prince of Wales, afterwards George IV. He infected young France with Anglomania in the form of horse-racing and hard drinking, and made himself popular among the lower classes by profuse charity.

In 1787 he showed his liberalism boldly against the King, and as the States-General drew near he lavished his wealth in flooding France with seditious books and papers. In the following year he promulgated his *Délibérations*, written by Laclos, to the effect that the Third Estate was the nation; and in June, 1789—the month that preceded the fall of the Bastille—he led the forty-seven nobles who seceded from their own order to join that Estate.

The Duke presumed to become constitutional King of France, or at least Regent; but he was only a comparatively small fragment that drifted into the vortex of the Revolution itself. In 1792, when all hereditary titles were swept away, this " citizen " adopted the name of Philippe Egalité.

He was the twentieth Deputy for Paris in the National Convention, and voted for the death of the King; but in the following year retribution overtook him, for he himself was found guilty of conspiracy and guillotined.

The public distrust of the King's party, the fatal error in bringing the foreign troops to Paris and its environs, and, finally, the banishment of Necker and the Duke of Orléans, the great champions of the people, must be regarded as the immediate cause of the catastrophe that followed.

CHAPTER VI

Madame Tussaud recalled from Versailles—The 12th of July, 1789—Busts taken from Curtius's Exhibition—A Garde Française slain in the mêlée.

IT must be remembered that the " romance " of Madame Tussaud's began in the French capital one hundred and fifty years ago.

As we view to-day the quaint little figure of Madame which stands in the Exhibition she helped to found in France and established in this country, we must imagine her in the full vigour of her young womanhood, sensible to the dangers and terrors of the Revolution in which she was about to be involved. The Exhibition was as yet in its infancy; but stirring times were approaching, and the days were pregnant with meaning for the France that was to be—a time of bloodshed and grim ruthlessness born of a people's desire for freedom, and attended by ghastly scenes in Paris that revealed the extremities to which unbridled human passions could go.

We must see through her eyes the sights that marked the red dawn of the French Revolution;

41

and hear the first low rumble that gave warning of the approach of the Reign of Terror. Her uncle recalled her from the Court of Versailles, in order that he might afford her his protection, and she did not leave a whit too soon.

Now we come to the fateful days of July.

The Three Estates had been fused into one on the 27th of June with the assent of the King, who thus virtually signed his own death-warrant. Another step soon followed in the same disastrous course. The Queen and her intimate advisers caused Louis to make an attempt to maintain his authority by force, and for this purpose an army of 40,000 men, drawn from various quarters, was concentrated upon Paris and its vicinity, and placed under the orders of Marshal Broglie.

Among these troops were several regiments of Swiss and Germans. At that moment Necker, whom the Court party distrusted and feared, was forced to relinquish his office, and commanded to leave France forthwith.

The 12th of July was a Sunday, and on the morning of that day an extraordinary degree of activity was observed among the troops in Paris. The nerves of the people became overwrought ; they were apprehensive of imminent danger— some hidden design, some sinister motive, on the part of the newly appointed Ministers (including the hated Foulon, who had succeeded the beloved Necker) whose policy they could not fathom.

Before midday the Palais Royal was crowded with people, wondering what all this military movement could mean, and gazing at the strange placards which bade them stay at home and avoid all meetings.

The half-discredited rumour of the dismissal of Necker spread like wild-fire through the capital, and the first person who made the announcement was about to be ducked in one of the water basins in the gardens of the Palais Royal, when a Deputy of the Third Estate, who happened to be standing by, confirmed the news.

Everyone in the gardens was at once made acquainted with the fall of the people's favourite ; and as the cannon of the Palais made known, as usual, the fact that the hour of noon had arrived, a young man named Camille Desmoulins sprang upon a table outside the Café Foy, and, brandishing a drawn sword and pistol, called " To arms ! " He then harangued with burning eloquence the people who crowded around him, and fired their imagination at the close of his oration by plucking a leaf from a tree (green being the colour of Necker's livery) and placing it in his hat as a cockade, an example that was followed by thousands.

The theatres and other places of amusement were closed as a sign of mourning for Necker, who was loudly acclaimed on every side.

Then it was suggested that the models of Necker

and the Duke of Orléans should be obtained from Curtius's Museum. The idea was quickly seized upon, and the crowd rushed *en masse* to the Exhibition rooms on the Boulevard du Temple, where they demanded the busts of the " friends of the people." They also asked for the model of the King, a request that was refused by Curtius, who observed that as the full-length figure was extremely heavy it would be " broken " if carried. This reply pleased the people, who clapped their hands and shouted " Bravo, Curtius, bravo ! "

Deeming it imprudent not to respond to the public clamour, Curtius relinquished the busts of the two public idols ; and as soon as they had gained possession of them the mob shouted " Long live Necker ! " " Long live the Duke of Orléans ! " and " Down with the foreign troops ! "

As an expression of grief at the loss of their favourites they covered the busts with crape. Then, elevating them upon pedestals, they carried them through the streets of Paris in triumph.

On rolled the procession through the Rue de Richelieu, the Boulevard, and the streets of St. Martin, St. Denis, and St. Honoré, increasing in numbers at every step, among them men of the Garde Française, till it came to the Place Vendôme, where the busts were carried twice round the statue of Louis XIV. *En route* the crowd obliged all they met to take off their hats in honour of the men the busts represented. By the time the great throng reached the Place Vendôme it had become 5,000 or 6,000 strong.

Here a detachment of royal troops came up, and vainly attempted to disperse the mob. The crowd pelted the soldiers with stones, and, having put them to flight, proceeded to the Place Louis XV., where they were assailed by the German troops of the Prince de Lambesc. The cavalry charged the mob with drawn sabres, and the bearers of the busts were thrown down beneath their burdens.

Again and again they were raised, only to fall once more. The figure of Necker was cleft asunder by a soldier of the Royal German Regiment. A man named Pepin, a hawker of articles of drapery, was wounded by a bullet in the leg, and fell by the side of the broken figure. That representing the Duke of Orléans escaped destruction ; but a member of the Civic Guard, while endeavouring to protect it, lost his life, and several other persons were wounded in attempting to assist him. It was the first blood shed in the Revolution, which may thus be regarded as having broken out at the very doors of the Exhibition in Paris.

Thomas Carlyle gives, in his *French Revolution*, the following characteristic account of the incident :

TO ARMS !
Sunday, 12th July, 1789.

France, so long shaken and wind-parched, is probably at the right inflammable point. As for poor Curtius, who, one grieves to think, might be but imperfectly paid, he cannot make two words about his Images. The Wax-bust of Necker, the Wax-bust of D'Orléans, helpers of France : these, covered with crape, as in funeral procession, or after the manner of suppliants appealing to Heaven, to Earth, and Tartarus itself, a mixed multitude bears off. For a sign ! As indeed man, with his singular imaginative faculties, can do little or nothing without signs : Thus Turks look to their Prophet's Banner ; also Osier *Mannikins* have been burnt, and Necker's Portrait has erewhile figured, aloft on its perch.

In this manner march they, a mixed, continually increasing multitude ; armed with axes, staves, and miscellanea ; grim, many-sounding through the streets. Be all Theatres shut ; let all dancing on planked floor, or on the natural greensward, cease ! Instead of a Christian Sabbath, and feast of *guinguitte* tabernacles, it shall be a Sorcerer's Sabbath ; and Paris, gone rabid, dance—with the Fiend for piper !

However, Besenval, with horse and foot, is in the Place Louis Quinze. Mortals promenading homewards, in the fall of the day, saunter by, from Chaillot or Passy, from flirtation and a little thin wine ; with sadder step than usual. Will the Bust-Procession pass that way ? Behold it ; behold also Prince Lambesc dash forth on it, with his Royal-Allemands ! Shots fall, and sabre-strokes ; Busts are hewed asunder ; and, alas, also heads of men. A sabred Procession has nothing for it but to *explode*, along what streets, alleys, Tuileries Avenues it finds ; and disappear. One unarmed man lies hewed down ; a Garde Française by his uniform ; bear him (or bear even the report of him) dead and gory to his Barracks ;—where he has comrades still alive !—*French Revolution*, Chapter IV.

It was on this very day, the 12th of July, after the incidents just described, that the famous reply was made to the King by Liancourt. Upon his apprising His Majesty of the ferment in Paris,

Louis remarked, "Why, it is a revolt, then?"
"No, sire," rejoined the Minister, "it is a
revolution!"[1]

---

[1] This reply has been erroneously asserted to have been made by
Liancourt on the evening of the 14th of July, the day of the capture
of the Bastille; it was really given as stated above.

CHAPTER VII

Heads of the Revolution—Madame's terrible experiences—The
guillotine in pawn—Madame acquires the knife, lunette,
and chopper.

IT is no part of our concern to trace the course of
the Revolution throughout, or to dwell too long
upon its horrors. Nevertheless before Madame
Tussaud passed into tranquil days she had to
suffer the severest ordeal of her life, the memory
of which she could never wholly efface.

We can hardly imagine her bitter experience
when compelled to employ her young hands in
taking impressions of heads immediately after
decapitation, and this, strange to say, by the very
same knife which may be seen at this day among the
relics of the Revolution at Tussaud's.

Thus she was compelled to reproduce the linea-
ments of Louis XVI., Marie Antoinette, Hébert,
Danton, Robespierre, Carrier, Fouquier-Tinville—
the best and fairest, and also the worst and vilest
—who met their death on the scaffold. Unthink-
able were the gruesome tasks of faithfully recording
their features imposed upon the young woman who

48

JEAN BAPTISTE CARRIER.
Impression of his head taken immediately after he had been
guillotined, 16th December, 1794.

[To face p. 48.

was destined to bring to England that Exhibition the annals of which we now relate.

No wonder many a heated controversy has waged around these works, for it is hard to realise that they are the actual impressions of those heads that fell under the knife of the guillotine. Yet they are the selfsame impressions that were shown at Christopher Curtius's Museum in Paris.

That Madame Tussaud's uncle would have had the temerity to exhibit spurious heads to a crowd by no means in a humour to be trifled with, and far too familiar with the features the casts portrayed to be deceived, is more than unlikely; and we know such an imposition in his case would have been quite unnecessary. The casts were undoubtedly taken under compulsion, either with the object of pandering to the temper of the people, or of serving as confirmatory evidence of execution having taken place—perhaps both.

The idea of exhibiting the heads of those who had been done to death as enemies of the people had asserted itself during the very earliest days of the Revolution. Within a fortnight of the taking of the Bastille, Foulon's head had been severed from its body and paraded through the streets of Paris at the end of a pike.

Later the noble features of the Princess de Lamballe had suffered the same brutal degradation, with the added inhumanity of having been thrust between the window-bars of the Temple Prison,

E

wherein the unfortunate Louis XVI. and his wife were incarcerated.

On that terrible day, the 10th of August, 1792, when the Swiss Guard was cut to pieces in defending the Tuileries, several of these brave soldiers had their heads stuck upon pikes and exhibited to the mob. The Royalist writer, Suleau, suffered the same fate.

How far had Madame Tussaud been implicated in the accomplishment of the dreadful work of taking casts from decapitated heads?

It was during the autumn of 1789 that Christopher Curtius (who had by this time adopted Marie as his daughter) insisted upon her withdrawing from the service of Madame Elizabeth, to whom she had, with every reason, become devotedly attached. For Curtius had, at the outset of the disturbances in Paris, espoused the cause of the people, and, as an adroit and far-seeing man, had become anxious for his adopted daughter's safety.

He, without doubt, desired she should return under his own roof to derive the benefit of his protection. So it is that we find Marie in her uncle's studio adjoining his Exhibition, and where that gruesome work was so soon to be undertaken.

Now during the year 1793 Curtius had been drawn into the service of the National Convention, and on several occasions had to quit Paris for many days at a time, leaving Marie and her mother to do the best they could with the Exhibition during

his absence. He was at this time " Envoy Extra-
ordinary of the Republic and War Commissary
at Mayence." On the last occasion of his quitting
the capital his absence extended over a period of
fully eighteen months.

Meanwhile heads were falling fast, and no
one knew how long his own would repose
upon his shoulders. Then it was that Marie
suffered the terrible experience of having to take
the impressions of so many heads that were brought
to her from the guillotine. We have it from her
own mouth that it was a task with which she dared
not hesitate to comply.

It must have been known to many that only a
few years back she had been a member of the
household of the King's sister, Madame Elizabeth,
at Versailles, and not a few of those who were
near and dear to her had suffered death for a far
less offence than that. But at last, as the days
wore on, the Jacobins themselves fell, and the
Reign of Terror gave way to the Directorate.
Then easier times came, though still far from
tranquil. Nevertheless heads had ceased to fall,
and Sanson, the executioner, finding his occupation
gone, pawned his guillotine, and got into woeful
trouble for alleged trafficking in municipal
property.

Years after Madame came to this country she
sent her son to Paris to search out this terrible
instrument of death, and, with the help of the

executioner, who was still living, and who solemnly vouched for its authenticity, she secured the knife, the lunette, and also the chopper that was used as a standby, lest the great knife should fail.

It was only after much negotiation and the payment of a very considerable sum of money that her object was attained. And now the dread knife harmlessly reposes by the side of the impressions of those heads it so ruthlessly struck off a century and a quarter ago—that of Louis XVI. and his Queen, Marie Antoinette, as well as those of Robespierre, Danton, Fouquier-Tinville, Hébert, and the miscreant of Nantes, Carrier. From the time they were first shown in Paris until the present day they have been viewed by an ever-increasing throng, though the sight of them can never have been pleasing, and those who gaze upon them shudder and pass on.

Though Madame Tussaud did not witness the execution of Marie Antoinette, yet she remembered seeing the Queen pass on a tumbril through the jeering crowds to the scaffold. The once gay and light-hearted Queen was dressed in white for her last pageant on earth, her hands tied behind her. The spectacle brought back to Madame memories of the royal palace where she had frequently attended to give lessons in modelling, and she was so overcome that she fainted. Perhaps the most horrifying experience undergone by Madame Tussaud during this terrible period was when the mangled head

MARIE ANTOINETTE.
Impression of her head taken immediately after she had been guillotined, 16th October, 1793.

[To face p. 52.

of the greatly beloved Princess de Lamballe was brought to her that a cast might be made. In vain did she protest that she could not endure the ordeal. The brutal murderers compelled her to comply.

CHAPTER VIII

ONE of the most bloodthirsty of all the red Terrorists was Jean Paul Marat, who was slain in his bath by Charlotte Corday on the 13th of July, 1793.

Marat, as a young man, had lived in this country for some time, and was well known to Madame Tussaud through visits he paid to the house of her uncle, Curtius, at 20 Boulevard du Temple.

Immediately after his assassination she was called upon to take a cast of Marat's head. " They came for me," she relates, " to go to Marat's house at once, and to take with me what appliances I needed to make an impression of his features. The cadaverous aspect of the fiend made me feel desperately ill, but they stood over me and forced me to perform the task." Marat's model is still to be seen in the Exhibition lying in the bath in which he was stabbed by the heroic young Norman girl.

JEAN PAUL MARAT.
Stabbed in his bath by Charlotte Corday, 13th July, 1793.

Charlotte Corday had addressed a letter to Marat stating that she had news of importance to communicate, and when she called he readily admitted her. She amused him with an account of the Deputies at Caen, when he said, " They shall all go to the guillotine." " To the guillotine ! " exclaimed she, and as he took up a pencil to write the names of his intended victims Charlotte plunged a knife into his heart.

Madame Tussaud afterwards visited Charlotte Corday in the Conciergerie Prison, and described her as tall, well-mannered, and possessed of many graces of character and appearance. The brave young woman, who paid for her avenging act with her life, wrote in a letter to her father that she had done what was right. After the heroine's death Madame Tussaud obtained a record of Charlotte Corday's beautiful face.

The actual model, now in our Exhibition, of Marat dying in his bath, was exhibited during the Revolution at the Museum of Curtius in Paris, and attracted crowds, who were loud in their lamentations, for at that time Marat was a national idol.

Robespierre visited the Museum, and took the opportunity of haranguing the people at the door. In flamboyant language he said, " Enter, citizens, and see the image of our departed friend, snatched from us by the assassin's hand, guided by the demon of aristocracy. Marat was the father of the poor, the defender of the weak, and the consoler of the wretched. As his heart poured forth the sweet emotions of sympathy for the oppressed, so did the vigour of his mind emit its thunder against the oppressor." Then, descending to bathos, the cunning demagogue exclaimed, " What did he get for it all? Five francs were found in his house ! "

Surprise has sometimes been expressed by visitors that the bath in which Marat was stabbed to death should be so small and of such a curious shape.

Marat was murdered in a " slipper " bath, which was more like a " half boot " than a slipper, so that the water would come up to the shoulders of the bather without flowing over. This kind of bath was greatly in vogue at the time of the French Revolution. Its object was to save water, which in those days was not freely supplied. When the bather was in the bath a small quantity of water would fill it.

Maximilien Robespierre had sent numerous people to their death during the Reign of Terror. His own turn came at last, when he too met his death from the sharp tongue of La Guillotine. The revulsion of feeling that had set in against Robespierre was very bitter. He was shot at point-blank range by a man named Meda in the Salle d'Egalité, a room in the Hôtel de Ville, but was only wounded, and he went to the guillotine on the 28th of July, 1794, with his broken jaw swathed in a white linen cloth.

MAXIMILIEN MARIE ISIDORE ROBESPIERRE.
Impression of his head taken immediately after he had been
guillotined, 28th July, 1794.

[To face p. 57.

An hour after the head of Robespierre rolled from the lunette Madame Tussaud, reluctantly obeying a demand that an impression should be taken of the severed head, set about the shuddering task. The cast therefrom is now shown in one of our Exhibition rooms containing relics of the Revolution. Her feelings may be imagined as she sat with the head of the callous Terrorist confronting her.

Although Madame Tussaud took an impression of the features of Robespierre directly after his execution, she had taken a portrait of him long before his fall. He expressed a wish that his figure should be introduced standing near that of Marat, as also those of Collot d'Herbois and Rosignol. He proposed that they should send their own clothes in which the figures might be dressed, to afford additional accuracy. The likenesses were taken and apparelled as desired.

In those days Madame Tussaud often sat next Robespierre at dinner. She describes him as always extremely polite and attentive, never omitting those little acts of courtesy which are expected from a gentleman when sitting at table with a lady, anticipating her wishes, and taking care that she should never have to ask for anything. In this particular, says Madame Tussaud, he differed from Marat, who was so selfishly eager to supply his own wants that he never troubled himself with the needs of others.

Robespierre's conversation was generally animated,

sensible, and agreeable, but his enunciation was
not good. There was nothing particularly remarkable in his conduct, manners, or appearance when
in society. If noticed at all, it could only be as
a pleasant, gentlemanly man of moderate abilities.
This was a strong admission for a lady who was
always a Royalist at heart and had been long
detained in Paris against her will.

Her association with the Court of Louis inevit-
ably brought Madame Tussaud under suspicion
of the so-called Committee of Public Safety, and
for a time she was imprisoned with Madame de
Beauharnais, who was later to become the Empress
Josephine, whom Napoleon divorced to marry
Marie Louise. The scene is changed, and we see
Marie Grosholtz—Curtius having died about that
time—wedded in 1795 to François Tussaud, by
whose name she was henceforth to be known to
posterity.

Madame Tussaud, it would appear, made the
acquaintance and gained the favour of Napoleon
himself.

A Parisian publication, *La Belle Assemblée*,
gives a circumstantial account of Madame Tussaud
being sent for to take the likeness of Napoleon
—when he was First Consul—at the Tuileries as
early as six o'clock in the morning. It would
appear that Madame went at the invitation of
Napoleon's first wife, Josephine, who was desirous
of having a permanent record of her husband's

features. The young modeller was ushered into a room at the palace where the great soldier waited for her. *La Belle Assemblée* states that Josephine greeted Madame Tussaud with kindness, and conversed much and most affably. Napoleon said little, spoke in sharp sentences, and rather abruptly.

He would have shown her special consideration had she chosen to remain in France ; but it is not to be wondered at that Madame Tussaud cared no longer to remain amid the sorrowful recollections of the Revolution, and that she seized the opportunity, on the signing of the Peace of Amiens, to leave France for ever. It was to England she turned for refuge and the prosecution of her life's work. Madame boldly transported across the Channel to England her uncle's two Paris Exhibitions, which, as already related, had been made into one. Here she decided to settle, and here her descendants have lived ever since.

CHAPTER IX

Madame Tussaud leaves France for England, never to return—
Early days in London—On tour—Some notable figures—
Shipwreck in the Irish Channel.

MADAME TUSSAUD arrived in this country with her Exhibition some time in May, 1802.

There is considerable difficulty in tracing her movements during the first few years after her arrival. The information points to her having remained in London with her Exhibition for some six or seven years. In London there is some amount of evidence of her having shown her exhibits in Fleet Street and also at the Lowther Arcade in the Strand.

However, it is fairly clear that she first showed her collection at the old Lyceum Theatre in the Strand, then known as the English Opera House, which she vacated in 1803 that Mr. Winsor might make the experiment of lighting the place with gas. It was the first house of entertainment to be illuminated in this way, and the innovation was regarded as dangerous.

Then she went on tour, and visited the more important places in England, Scotland, and Ireland.

MADAME TUSSAUD
at the age of 42,
when she left France for England

(*A Portrait Study by John T. Tussaud*)

[To face p. 60.

Wherever the town visited boasted a Mayor, the Exhibition was almost invariably opened by him, or under his auspices.

The figures that Madame Tussaud modelled and the dates when she executed the work give some idea of her activities at the time.

She modelled from life Queen Caroline in 1808, George III. in 1809, and Alexander I., Emperor of Russia, in 1814. In that year the Emperor and the King of Prussia visited England in connection with the centenary of the House of Hanover, which took place on the 1st of August.

Madame Tussaud also modelled from life Mrs. Siddons, the famous actress, who retired from the stage in 1809, and died at her residence in Upper Baker Street in 1831.

* Princess Charlotte of Wales (daughter of George IV.) was married on the 2nd of May, 1816, and on that day Her Royal Highness sat to Mr. P. Turnerelli, the sculptor, for what was called " the Nuptial Bust." From this Madame Tussaud modelled a figure of the Princess for the Exhibition, and it drew large numbers of people to see it when the young Princess died in the year following her marriage.

> For blooming Charlotte, England's fairest Rose,
> In History's page the tear of pity flows.
> Few were the moments of connubial life,
> She shar'd the blisses of a happy wife.
> But when relentless Death had nipt her bloom,
> And hid the faded Rose within the tomb,

O'er her cold grave an Angel waved his wing,
And cried, " O Death, where is thy fatal sting ?
From hence she goes ; to me the charge is given,"
And in his bosom took the Rose to Heaven.

The Duke of York was modelled from life in
1812, Leopold I., King of Belgium, in 1817, the
Bishop of Norwich in 1820, and George IV. a few
days before his coronation in July, 1821. Sir
Walter Scott's figure in Highland costume was
taken from life in Edinburgh in 1828, a year after
George Canning's likeness had been similarly
obtained.

It was in 1828 that Madame Tussaud took a
portrait of the miscreant Burke, immediately
after his execution ; and she modelled from life
his accomplice, Hare, while he was in prison in
Edinburgh.

Prince Talleyrand's figure was modelled from
life by Madame in 1832, Lord Eldon in 1833, the
Duke of Wellington and Sir Robert Peel in 1835,
and Lord Melbourne in 1836.

In that year Madame Tussaud took from life a
model of the Duchess of Kent, the mother of
Queen Victoria, which proved a great attraction.
By this time the Exhibition had found a home
in Baker Street, where it became established in
the spring of 1835.

Concerning the travels of the Exhibition, it is
on record that Madame Tussaud visited North
Shields on the 2nd of December, 1811, and

Edinburgh in 1811-12. Early in the latter year we find her on the 28th of February at " 4 The Market Place, Hull, just opposite the Reindeer Inn." She was in Leeds on the 28th of September, and in Manchester on the 2nd of December, 1812. There is an entry in an old account-book which says, " Left the house in Criggate, Leeds, Monday, November 16." It is pretty clear that the Exhibition was located in Newcastle in January, and in Liverpool on the 13th of April, 1813.

In 1817 the Exhibition was shown at " Mr. Sparrow's Upper Ware Rooms, Old Butter Market, Ipswich, having lately arrived from the Concert Rooms, Canterbury, and lastly from the Assembly Rooms, Deal."

It was probably when the Exhibition was visiting Cambridge in 1818 that a worthy Don made the suggestion that the figures of criminals should be placed in a separate room. Too long would be taken even to name all the places that were visited by the Exhibition, but there is an account in the *Coventry Herald* that on the 14th March, 1823, the cordial thanks of a meeting of school managers were presented to Madame Tussaud for her " unsolicited and handsome donation of a moiety of the receipts of her Exhibition on Monday evening last."

Among the figures taken on tour at this time were models of Louis XVI., Marie Antoinette, and the Dauphin, Voltaire, and Madame St. Amaranthe

(Tussaud's " Sleeping Beauty "), taken a few months before her execution. These identical figures, as already stated, are still in the collection.

To trace the travels of the Exhibition there is no need. For some years Madame, with her sons, Joseph and Francis, went on tour throughout the country. A misadventure in the Irish Channel, when she was on her way to Dublin, threatened the enterprise with disaster. The vessel which carried their precious belongings was partially wrecked, and many valuable exhibits were lost. Undaunted by the buffetings of Fate, and helped by friends, Madame replenished her Exhibition and brought it up to date.

The current of events did not run smoothly for Madame Tussaud ; but the little woman possessed a brave spirit, and struggled on against adversity, being upheld by the conviction that she would eventually triumph.

CHAPTER X

THE Bristol riots in the autumn of 1831 brought the
Exhibition into serious jeopardy. Madame Tussaud
had just arrived in the city of the West Country, when
the Recorder, Sir Charles Wetherell, came to open a
Special Commission for the trial of certain political
offenders associated with the agitation for reform.
Judge Wetherell was heartily disliked by West-
country folk, and there was strong opposition to this
Special Commission being held. Public resentment
developed into a riot, which the military was sent to
subdue.

Madame tells the story herself of the sufferings she
endured during the days of wanton destruction and
loss of life, as the rabble resorted to killing and
pillage. Judge Wetherell was obliged to escape from
the city, disguising himself, as it was then stated,
with some taunt at his personal habits, " through
the medium of a wash and the donning of a clean
shirt and collar."

The three days' terror can scarcely be considered
the result of a genuine revolutionary movement.
True, certain ringleaders of the rabble seem to have

imagined in some vague way that they were hastening the day of " liberty " ; but the rioters only
destroyed for sheer destruction's sake.   What they
sought to promote they neither knew nor cared.
For the most part the mob was utterly contemptible,
and but for the extraordinary apathy of the
authorities the riot might have been easily
quelled.

It was on the morning of Saturday, the 29th of
October, that the Recorder came to the city, and,
a disturbance being feared, a number of special
constables were sworn in.   These officials, mostly
young men, did more harm than good, for they
irritated the people by overmuch zeal, and led to
blows being exchanged, which fomented the trouble.
This was followed by an attack on the Mansion
House, where Sir Charles was banqueting with the
Corporation.

The civic party was hunted out, and made its
escape over the housetops.   Suddenly the cry was
raised, " To the back ! " and the mob surged round
to the offices behind the Mansion House, where
faggots and firewood were stored.   For the present
the rioters refrained from firing the building, and
contented themselves with looting the premises.
The cellars proved particularly attractive to the
unruly crowd, which was shortly in possession of a
hundred dozen of wine, and the day closed amid
general drunkenness and disorder.

On Sunday morning the mob reassembled in Queen

Square. The authorities had plucked up sufficient courage to publish a proclamation warning all rioters to return to their homes ; but these gentlemen were not disposed to take the admonition seriously. The unlucky bill-sticker who posted the proclamation was badly mauled.

One individual mounted King William's statue in the Square and waved a tricoloured cap on a pole, shouting to his comrades to behold the cap of Liberty. Possibly this aroused in the minds of the befuddled rioters some recollection of the French Revolution, for a move was made towards the gaol, which was speedily in their power. A vigorous employment of sledge-hammers soon broke in the prison doors, and the prisoners, some of them almost nude, at once joined the mob.

The Governor's house was sacked and fired ; his books were pitched into the New River, and the prison van met with a similar fate. Then the Gloucester County Gaol, the lock-up house at Lawford's Gate, and the Bishop's Palace were all fired. Between seven and eight o'clock the rioters revisited the cellars of the Mansion House and began rolling out barrels of beer and wine. Intoxicated persons could be seen moving about the kitchen and the banqueting-room with lighted candles, and in less than two hours the building was gutted.

Dwellings in Queen Square were sacked and fired, until the whole mass was wrapped in flames. Such was the remarkable lethargy of the householders that a few mischievous boys made a house-to-house visitation, gave the inmates half an hour's notice to quit, and at the expiration of that time coolly set fire to the houses without molestation. The booty the rioters seized was trifling. On the corpse of one boy, who was sabred by a soldier, was found a curious collection of spoil—a lady's glove, some children's books, and the Custom House keys.

One curious incident happened when the contents of fifty puncheons of rum gushed out of a bonded warehouse and ran flowing down the street, setting fire to a house at the other end.

The riots were quelled by the military on the Monday, after many thousands of pounds' worth of property had been destroyed ; and one of the results was that four persons were hanged.

By what might almost be described as a stroke of good fortune—inasmuch as it perpetuated the name of Tussaud—there was in Bristol at that time a lad of nineteen years, named William Muller, whose genius as a painter gives Bristol just cause for pride to-day. This gifted youth produced a series of wonderful sketches of the " Bristol Revolution," as it was then called, in which he portrays the weird and striking scenes of incendiarism in the city streets.

One of these sketches is now in our possession. It shows Madame Tussaud's Exhibition premises standing out full and clear in the fiery glare, while the figures and other articles are being hurriedly re-moved and piled up in the roadway before the jeering

THE BRISTOL RIOTS

showing the figures being removed for security from the Exhibition
premises, Sunday, 30th October, 1831.

(*From a water-colour drawing made on the spot by William Muller*)

[To face p. 68.

mob. The figures and decorations are easily recognised in the picture, and many of them are still included in the Exhibition.

For no imaginable reason the premises occupied by Madame Tussaud's collection had been marked to be burnt. A chalk sign was scrawled upon the door, and the adjoining buildings, besmeared with petroleum, had been already set on fire. In Madame's employment was a stalwart and loyal negro. This black servant took up his position at the entrance to the Exhibition, and threatened to kill with a blunderbuss the first man who dared approach to harm the place.

The negro kept the mob at bay long enough, it would seem, to save the building, for at eight o'clock Madame's anxiety was relieved when she heard, above the wild yelling of the infuriated people, the distant sounds of the drums and fifes of the 11th Infantry Regiment, just then reaching the outskirts of the city. The music that cheered her scared the plundering rabble and stayed their depredations.

Madame Tussaud came through all this in her seventieth year, with twenty years of activity still before her; and, after a long tour through provincial towns, she took her Exhibition to Blackheath, on the south-eastern side of London, attracted, no doubt, by the fact that that place had become a fashionable resort owing to the residence there, some years previously, of Queen Caroline, the estranged wife of George IV.

CHAPTER XI

An old placard now in our possession informs us that at Blackheath the Exhibition was housed in the Assembly Room at the Green Man Hotel. The exact date when it left there is not known, but we do know that it had previously found a temporary abode in the Town Hall, Brighton.

There it was visited early in 1833 by members of the Royal Family, then in residence at the Pavilion, as is vouched for in the following quaint notice. The placard we give in full, not only on account of its quaint wording, but because it gives a good idea of the Exhibition as it then existed :

NOW OPEN!

WITH DECIDED SUCCESS!

The Promenade being Crowded every Evening !

In the only Room that could be had sufficiently spacious for the purpose,

The GREAT ASSEMBLY ROOM of the late

70

ROYAL LONDON BAZAAR,
GRAY'S INN ROAD
(Which has been fitted up for the purpose). Carriages may wait in the Arena.

Lately arrived from the Town Hall, Brighton, and last from the Assembly Room, Green Man Hotel, Blackheath.

SPLENDID NOVELTY,
Coronation Groups and Musical Promenade.

ENTIRELY NEW.

MADAME TUSSAUD AND SONS

Have the honor to announce that their entirely new Exhibition, which has only to be seen to ensure its support and patronage, justly entitling it to the appellation of the most popular Collection in the Empire, is NOW OPEN as above mentioned, and they trust the Public will not form their ideas of it from anything of a similar description they may have seen in this Metropolis or elsewhere—as in their peculiar art they stand alone ; a fact acknowledged by those that have made the tour of Europe. They are induced to state this to guard against the prejudice excited by a view of inferior Collections. Madame Tussaud had the honor of being Artist to Her Royal Highness Madame Elizabeth, was patronized by the late Royal Family of France, by their Royal Highnesses the Duke and Duchess of York, twice by the Universities of Oxford and Cambridge, and lately at the Town Hall, Brighton, by Her Royal Highness the Princess Augusta, His Royal Highness Prince George, and by nearly the whole of the Royal Establishment.

Her Royal Highness, with that kindness which has ever distinguished the Royal Family for the encouragement of the Fine Arts, honored Madame Tussaud with the following letter :

" Lady Mary Taylor is commanded by Her Royal Highness the Princess Augusta to acquaint Madame Tussaud with Her Royal Highness's approbation of her Exhibition, which is well worthy of admiration, and the view of which afforded Her Royal Highness much amusement and gratification.—Pavilion, Brighton, Feb. 9, 1833."

The placard goes on to describe the Exhibition as follows :

> The Exhibition consists of a great variety of Public Characters, modelled with the greatest care, and regardless of expense, among whom will be noticed the original figures of BURKE and HARE (taken from their faces, to obtain which the Proprietors went expressly to Scotland) ; which have excited intense interest from the peculiar nature of their crimes, and their approach to life, which renders it difficult to recognize them from living persons. Also DENNIS COLLINS (taken from life at the gaol, Reading), in the identical dress he had on when he made the atrocious attempt on His Majesty's life at Ascot Heath Races.

This shows that Madame Tussaud in those days, as her successors do in these, took the greatest pains to ensure fidelity as regards costume as well as features.

There can be no doubt that Madame Tussaud actually originated the promenade concerts which have since become so popular a form of musical entertainment, for the placard goes on to announce that :

> There will be a Musical Promenade every Evening from Half-past Seven till Ten, when a selection of Music will be performed by the Messrs. Tussaud and Fishers ; the Promenade will be lighted with a profusion of lamps, producing, with the variety of rich costumes, special decorations, etc., an unequalled *coup d'œil*.

A description is next given of some of the exhibits, which will be perused with interest :

> The Collection consists of PORTRAITS in composition as large as life, dressed in appropriate costumes.

FIRST—GROUP REPRESENTING THE CORONATION OF H.M. WILLIAM IV.

Description.—It represents HIS MAJESTY on the Throne, habited in his Robes of State, as worn on that august occasion, in the act of being Crowned by the Archbishop of Canterbury, supported by the Bishop of Norwich. On His Majesty's right, Her Majesty QUEEN ADELAIDE, wearing the Cap of State, supported by Earl Grey, in his Coronation Robes. On His Majesty's left, the Lord Chancellor Brougham and the Duke of Wellington, in their Coronation Robes, surmounted by Three allegorical Figures representing Britannia, Caledonia, and Hibernia.

SECOND GROUP.
THE CORONATION OF BUONAPARTE,
Copied from the Celebrated Picture by David.

Description.—The moment chosen is the time when Buonaparte, contrary to all precedent, crowned himself. It represents him in the act of placing the Crown on his head, dressed in the magnificent costume as worn by him at his Coronation ; also a Figure of the Empress Josephine, who is seen kneeling at the foot of the altar, accompanied by a Page. At the altar is represented His Holiness Pope Pius VI., giving the benediction, supported by the celebrated Cardinal Fesche (Buonaparte's Uncle) and Prince Roustan (Buonaparte's favourite Mameluke) in the act of pro claiming the ceremony, attended by a Mameluke.

The two above-mentioned Groups have been universally admired by every one that has seen them ; and Madame Tussaud and Sons hope they will meet with the approbation of the Inhabitants of London and its Vicinity.

NEW GROUP taken from the History of Scotland.
MARY QUEEN OF SCOTS ABDICATING THE THRONE.

Description.—It represents her at the moment of hesitating to abdicate, being alarmed at the conduct of Baron Ruthven, who stands opposite to her. Next to him is the Figure of Sir J. Melville, interceding to appease the Baron ; and behind the Queen is a venerable Figure of an Augustin Monk, who is in the attitude of indignation at seeing his Mistress insulted.

Characters as follows—Full-length models :

HIS LATE MAJESTY GEORGE THE FOURTH.
Her late Majesty Queen Caroline.
Her late R.H. Princess Charlotte.
Their Majesties George III. and Queen Charlotte.
HIS LATE ROYAL HIGHNESS THE DUKE OF YORK.
Field-Marshall the Duke of Wellington.
His late Imperial Majesty Alexander of Russia ; and
HIS MAJESTY the KING of the BELGIANS.
FIELD MARSHALL VON BLUCHER.
Right Honorable WILLIAM PITT.
Right Honorable GEORGE CANNING.
Right Honorable C. J. FOX.
Reverend JOHN WESLEY.
The Celebrated QUEEN ELIZABETH.
The Immortal SHAKSPEARE.
WILLIAM PENN, founder of Pennsylvania.
MARY QUEEN OF SCOTS.
AN AUSTIN MONK.
BARON RUTHVEN.
LORD MELVILLE.
The celebrated BARON EMANUEL SWEDENBORG.

CHAPTER XII

THE old placard next proceeds to enumerate some of the then modern celebrities in the Exhibition as follows :

Portrait likeness of the Rev. John Clowes, of St. John's Church, Manchester, and late Fellow of Trinity College, Cambridge, taken (with permission) from life within the last ten years ; the Artist, Mr. J. P. Kemble, in the character of Hamlet ; the celebrated Mrs. Siddons in the character of Queen Catherine ; Dey of Algiers ; full-length Portrait of Daniel O'Connell, esq., M.P., taken with permission (from Mr. P. Turnerelli's celebrated bust), for which Mr. O'Connell gave sittings in Dublin ; Sir Walter Scott, taken from life in Edinburgh, by Madame Tussaud, which was seen by thousands, and also honored by his approbation ; Lord Byron, taken from life in Italy.

The other subjects comprising this unique exhibition, consisting of Characters in full dress as large as life, correctly executed, may be classed as follows:

The late Royal Family of France, taken from life, viz., the King, Queen, and Dauphin ; Pope Pius VI., Henry IV. of France, Duc de Sully, M. Voltaire, Napoleon Buonaparte, Madame Josephine Buonaparte, Cardinal Fesche, one of Buonaparte's Mameluke Guards, and Prince Roustan, Buonaparte's favorite Mameluke.

75

REMARKABLE CHARACTERS, SUBJECTS, &c.

An old Coquette, who teased her husband's life out. Two beautiful Infants. A small cabinet of Portraits in wax by the celebrated Courcius of Paris, viz., the Dying Philosopher, Socrates. Death of Cleopatra, Queen of Egypt. M. Voltaire. Shepherd and Shepherdess.

Biographical and descriptive Sketches may be had at the place of Exhibition, price Sixpence each.

Madame TUSSAUD and SONS, in offering this little notice to the Public, have endeavoured to blend utility and amusement. It contains an outline of the history of each character represented in the Exhibition, which will not only greatly increase the pleasure to be derived from a mere view of the figures, but will also convey to the minds of young persons much biographical knowledge, a branch of education universally allowed to be one of the highest importance.

ADMITTANCE 1s. CHILDREN *under* 8 *Years of Age* 6d. ; second room 6d.

Tickets for Six Weeks, not transferable, 5s. Open every day from 11 till 4 o'clock, in the Evening from 7 till 10.

The following highly interesting figures and objects, in consequence of the Peculiarity of their appearance, are placed in an adjoining situation, and are well worth the attention of artists and amateurs, taken by order of the National Assembly by Madame Tussaud—The Celebrated John Marat, one of the leaders of the French Revolution, taken immediately after his assassination by Charlotte Corde. The following heads—Robespiere, Carrier, Fouquier de Tainville, and Herbert were taken immediately after execution. The celebrated Count de Lorge, who was confined twenty years in the Bastile, taken from life. Mirabeau. Also, Phrenological Portraits of

STEWART AND HIS WIFE,

Who were executed in Edinburgh on the 13th of August, 1829, having confessed to the murder of Seven Persons by means of Poison, which they familiarly called doctoring.

CASTS OF CORDER AND HOLLOWAY, taken from their faces.

CURIOUS AND INTERESTING RELICS, &c.

The shirt of Henry IV. of France in which he was assassinated by Ravaillac, with various original documents relative to that transaction. A small model of the original French Guillotine, with its apparatus. Model of the Bastile in Paris in its entire state.

AN EGYPTIAN MUMMY.

Proved by the Hieroglyphics to be the body of the Princess of Memphis, who lived in the time of Sesostris, King of Egypt, a.m. 2528, 1491 years before Christ, being actually 3328 years old.

(PHAIR, Printer, 67, Great Peter Street, Westminster.)

A further placard is headed as follows :

REMOVAL POSTPONED TILL FURTHER NOTICE.

The Flattering Success with which this Exhibition continues to be honored, (the Promenade being Crowded every Evening), the very general desire expressed by Thousands for it to remain some time longer, (its merits becoming more generally known), being acknowledged to be the most Splendid, and, at the same time, the most Instructive to Youth, (induces the Proprietors to obey the general wish.) It will remain in consequence till further Notice.

The Exhibition is, therefore, located in " The Great Assembly Room of the late Royal London Bazaar, Gray's Inn Road." There it remained till early in March, 1835, on the 21st of which month it removed to its quarters in Baker Street.

As for the Assembly Room, it appears that on Tuesday, the 29th of March, directly after Madame Tussaud left, it was put up for sale at the Mart by the famous auctioneer, George Robins.

A lady, on viewing the Exhibition when it was in Gray's Inn Road, wrote the following excellent verses :

I stand amid a breathless throng,
　　Though animation's light is here ;
Expression, too, that might belong
　　To creatures of a nobler sphere ;
Where'er I turn my dazzled view,
I marvel what Art's hand can do !

Here are the lips, and cheeks, and eyes,
　　The folded hands—the beaming brow—
Those graces Nature's self supplies—
　　All burst upon my vision now !
And is it FICTION ?—can it be
That these are not *reality*?

The eye, where centres Genius' light ;
　　The lips, where Eloquence presides ;—
The cheek with Beauty's roses bright ;
　　The breast, where Passion darkly hides ;
The Warrior's pride, the Cynic's sneer,
From Nature's book are copied here !

PAINTING her meed of praise may claim
　　From Fame's proud trump or Minstrel's lyre,
And around SCULPTURE'S gifted name
　　May burn the POET'S words of fire ;
But TUSSAUD !　Both these arts divine
Must yield in *novelty* to THINE.

Thou bring'st before our wond'ring eyes,
　　Modell'd in truth, each gone-by scene
That Hist'ry's varied page supplies ;—
　　Here still *they* flourish, fresh and green,
Defying Time's oblivious power,
Who long have pass'd Life's fitful hour.

Modern Prometheus ! who can'st give,
  ike him of old, to human form
All *but* the life ;—here THOU wilt live
  And triumph o'er the " creeping worm "
That sullies all things—pale Decay !
Thy features ne'er can pass away ![1]

A nobler Trophy far is thine,
  Than " storied urn," by stranger hands,
Rear'd (in thy now adopted clime),
  And higher reverence commands ;
These forms—to which thine Art has lent
Life's truth—shall be THY MONUMENT !
               MRS. CORNWELL BARON-WILSON.

It is interesting to note that one of the first visitors to the Exhibition in its settled home at Baker Street was the great Duke of Wellington. He was there on Wednesday, the 26th of August, and after that date was frequently to be seen walking through the rooms, his favourite models being those of Queen Victoria and the dead Napoleon.

Indeed, the Duke requested Mr. Joseph Tussaud, the elder son of Madame Tussaud, to let him know whenever a new figure of exceptional interest was added to the Exhibition—*not forgetting the Chamber of Horrors.*

Mr. Tussaud ventured a remark expressing his surprise that the Duke should be interested in such figures, whereupon the old warrior turned upon him with the rejoinder, " Well, do they not represent *fact* ? "

[1] Alluding to the exquisite figure of the artist's self.

Other models added about this time included those of Nicholas I. of Russia, Louis Philippe, King of the French, the Duke of Cumberland, Talleyrand, and Hume, the historian.

A tragic occurrence took place shortly after the Exhibition had taken up its abode in London, and led to its permanent establishment in the Metropolis. At that time Madame de Malibran, the eldest daughter of the Spanish singer, Manuel Garcia, was idolised by the populace as a gifted songstress. She died suddenly during a festival held at Manchester on the 23rd of September, 1836, in the twenty-eighth year of her age.

Madame Tussaud placed her figure in the Exhibition with all speed, and the numerous admirers of the *prima donna* flocked to see it. The idea there and then took hold of Madame Tussaud's mind that the Exhibition would command perennial success by being constantly brought up to date through the adding of the portraits of people whose names were on everybody's lips. This principle has been faithfully observed ever since.

In the early days at Baker Street " the Hours of Exhibition," as the Catalogue quaintly puts it, were " from 11 in the Morning till 5, and from 7 in the Evening till 10. Brilliantly illuminated at 8." When the place was closed, seats were provided in the vestibule, and it was no uncommon sight to see from fifty to a hundred persons waiting for the reopening of the doors at 7 p.m.

" In part payment of a bad debt ! " Who the debtor was, there is no telling now ; it is, however, known that the carriage had been bought at a Tattersall auction, when short-sighted speculators let Napoleon's chariot go cheap.

Previously the carriage had earned a fortune for Mr. William Bullock, who took it round the country as an exhibit, which the people flocked in their thousands to see, till the novelty wore off and the carriage was rolled into the repository of Jeffreys, the coach-builder, where it remained for years with none to do it reverence. A cartoon in *Punch* by Cruikshank, in November of the Waterloo year, portrays a clamorous crowd surrounding the carriage when on view at the Egyptian Hall, and, it must be admitted, treating it with scant respect.

The carriage had been sent as a present to George IV. when Prince Regent, and in due time it arrived at Carlton House with four high-stepping Normandy horses. *Blackwood's Magazine* of March, 1817, states that " Bonaparte's military carriage has excited more interest as an exhibit than anything for a number of years." The manner in which the four horses were driven through the city by the French coachman, Jean Hornn, who lost his right arm when the carriage was captured, proves the excellent manner in which the horses were broken in. Mr. Bullock, in whose hands this splendid trophy of victory was placed by the Government, is said to have cleared £26,000 by his exhibition of it.

There is a letter in existence by Mr. William Bullock in which he states that

> . . . the celebrated Carriage, taken by the Prussian troops about fifteen miles from Waterloo on the evening of the great Battle, was afterwards purchased by me from his late Majesty George IV. for the sum of £2,500, and exhibited by me at the Egyptian Hall, Piccadilly, London, as well as in the principal Cities in Great Britain and Ireland, by the Authority of the Government, and is the identical carriage I have just seen in your possession. The Diamonds found in the Carriage . . . were purchased by Mr. Mawe, diamond merchant in the Strand, from Baron Von Keller, the Officer that captured them. The present one, with others, was purchased by me from Mr. Mawe.
>
> I am, Dear Sir,
> Your most obedient Servant,
> WILLIAM BULLOCK.

It is not known what Mr. Joseph Tussaud paid Mr. Robert Jeffreys, the Gray's Inn Road coach-builder, for it ; but this much may be said, that the carriage which proved so good an investment for Mr. Bullock has fulfilled all expectations at Madame Tussaud's, where it is pre-eminently the right thing in the right place.

It was certified at the time that M. Simon, of Brussels, built the carriage, and that most of the contrivances for economising space and ensuring comfort and convenience were suggested by the Emperor himself and his second wife, Marie Louise ; also that this was the carriage which picked up

Napoleon on his retreat to Paris after the burning of Moscow.

Scarcely less singular than the coincidence of my great-uncle meeting with the countryman on London Bridge was my acquiring, sixteen years ago, from a second-hand bookseller in Margate, an original official letter relating to the carriage. The letter, it will be seen, bears a date about five months after the Battle of Waterloo. It reads :

Downing Street,
27th Nov., 1815.

SIR,

I am directed by Lord Bathurst to request that you would receive into the King's Mews the travelling carriage of General Bonaparte, together with all its appurtenances, and also the four horses and the harness taken from the same, and keep them from public view till further notice.

I have the honour to be, Sir,
Your most obedient humble servant,
HENRY GOULBURN.

William Parker, Esqre., &c., &c., &c.,
Royal Mews.

The following affidavit sworn by Jean Hornn at the Mansion House before the famous Lord Mayor, Sir Matthew Wood, on the 9th of March, 1816, is of peculiar interest, containing as it does several important historic details :

AFFIDAVIT OF JEAN HORNN.

JEAN HORNN, a native of Bergen-op-Zoom in Holland, and now of Piccadilly in the County of Middlesex, aged twenty-eight years, maketh oath :—

THAT about ten years ago he entered into the service of Napoleon Bonaparte, the late Emperor of France, and attended Napoleon, in the capacity of his military coach-man, through the campaign which was distinguished by the battle of Jena—

THAT he attended Napoleon, in the same capacity of military coachman, during the subsequent campaigns, through the greater part of Prussia, Spain, Germany, and Russia, and in his excursion to Italy—

AND this Deponent saith, that he drove the military Carriage of the said Ex-Emperor from Paris to Waterloo ; in which Carriage the Emperor travelled thither, accom-panied by General Bertrand—

THAT on the evening of the day on which the battle of Waterloo was fought, he, this Deponent, was attacked, while with the said Carriage, by a detachment of Prussian lancers, and other infantry, who captured the Carriage, together with the Necessaire, and other articles it contained for the personal use of the Ex-Emperor—

THAT whilst this Deponent was remaining with the Carriage, in a field about thirty paces from the road, en-deavouring to pass round Jenappe (which was blocked up in the confusion of the retreat) he, this Deponent, received ten wounds in various parts of the body ; three of which were in his right arm—

THAT having then no appearance of life, he was left among the dead—

THAT a few days afterwards, and whilst this Deponent was lying in great agony at Jenappe, he was removed by a British officer ; who conveyed him to Brussels, and who obtained the amputation of this Deponent's arm, as well as surgical care of his other wounds—

THAT he afterwards returned to Paris ; and has received from the present Government of France a small annual pension—

AND this Deponent saith, that he hath inspected the Carriage, Horses, Necessaire of Gold and Silver, their respective Cases, the Pistols, Wearing Apparel, and other Articles now exhibiting at the London Museum, in Piccadilly (and which this Deponent hath been informed have been received there from the British Government), and that they are the same Carriage, Horses, Necessaire, and other

Articles which belonged to the late Emperor of France, and were personally used by him—

AND that the Carriage is the same in which the Ex-Emperor proceeded to Moscow; and which Carriage was driven by this Deponent, with the Ex-Emperor therein, twenty-four leagues beyond that City, on the road to Chotillowo—

THAT after the French army evacuated Moscow, and in the retreat toward France, the same Carriage was removed from off the perch and wheels, and placed on a sledge, and that the Ex-Emperor travelled therein, and was driven by this Deponent—

AND this Deponent also saith, that he hath seen and examined the Grey Surtout Coat, lined with Sable Fur, which is also at the London Museum; and that it is the same which this Deponent hath frequently seen worn by the said Ex-Emperor during the Russian campaign; and that the parts of the coat which appear to have been burnt and scorched were chiefly so burnt and scorched by the fires, before which it was frequently placed during that campaign—

AND this Deponent saith, that the Fur Travelling Cap, and the several other Articles of Wearing Apparel (exclusive of those which came from the British Government, and which are also at the London Museum) were parts of the personal Wardrobe of the Ex-Emperor of France; and were frequently used and worn by him—

AND this Deponent was present when the said Surtout Coat, Travelling Cap, and other last-mentioned Articles were purchased by Mr. Bullock, at Paris, of Guste Maitrot, who was keeper of the Wardrobe to the late Emperor of France.

JEAN HORNN.

Sworn at the Mansion House, London, the 9th day of March, 1816; having been first interpreted to the Deponent, JEAN HORNN, by ADAM BRIEFF, who was sworn duly to interpret and explain the same to him.

Before me, MATTHEW WOOD, Mayor.

CHAPTER XIV

Napoleon's Waterloo carriage—Description of its exterior.

SOME account must be given of this most interesting relic.

Ever since it first came to the Exhibition it has excited the most lively interest, and, until it was covered in by a glazed case, visitors enjoyed the privilege of sitting inside—a proceeding which would not have mattered had not unscrupulous souvenir hunters abused this favour by pilfering portions of the fabric that lined it.

Time-worn, it now stands before us, a thing of gaunt and sombre aspect. This old war-coach offers, to those who contemplate it, a full measure of historic reminiscence, recalling the most striking and critical episodes in the great Corsican's career.

He entered it at the time his power stood at its zenith, and retained it in constant attendance upon him down to the hour he took refuge within it, a conquered and a broken man. It was built for his campaign in Russia. In it he travelled many a league on the road to Moscow. Bereft of its

JOSEPH TUSSAUD.
Elder son of Madame
Tussaud.
Born 1796 ; died 1864.

NAPOLEON'S MILITARY CARRIAGE.
Captured on the retreat from Waterloo.

wheels and lashed upon a sleigh, through the perils of that terrible retreat, it safely carried him far on his way back to the gates of Paris. With him it was sent to the Isle of Elba ; thence it helped him along on his last auspicious journey to the French capital.

It assisted him on his way to Waterloo. Standing on the main road hard by La Belle Alliance, it awaited him throughout that memorable Sunday, the 18th of June, over a hundred years ago. At the end of the day's ordeal into it, sore and ill, he flung himself, only to struggle from it at the point of capture to take refuge in the confusion and the shadow of the night, leaving his hat, sword, and many other things behind him.

Deepened long ago into a monotone of dusky grey, still here and there the old coach betrays a touch of colour, revealing a fair estimate of its former self. Simple and modest as Imperial carriages go, nevertheless, on a certain May day in the year 1812, as it sallied forth on its maiden voyage, its back turned upon the old Palace of St. Cloud and its fore-carriage set upon the highroad to Russia, it must have looked a comely chariot—as yet unsullied by the stain of travel, and not yet degraded by the lust of war.

By the man that made it—one Simon, of Brussels, to whom reference has already been made—it would have been designated a *berline de voyage*, or maybe a *carrosse a six chevaux* ; by us it has been called a travelling carriage, and technically classed as a chariot-built coach.

Dark-blue, black, and yellow, with here and there a line of red and gold, were the colours under which it made its début.

The head, or upper part of the body, is constructed of thick black-enamelled leather, stretching over a strong framework of ash. The lower portion consists of finely polished wood panelling, originally of a rich dark-blue colour. A narrow brass fillet traverses the centre of the body, lining off its upper from its lower sections, and under this fillet runs a delicate gilt scroll composed of the fruit, leaf, and tendrils of the vine. This neat and unpretentious bordering, together with the emblazonment of the Imperial arms upon the doors, constitutes the only tangible claim the carriage has to anything in the nature of artistic adornment.

A curious bulkhead, or boot, built out from the forepart of the coach, provides, among other things, the very important accommodation contingent upon a long and unbroken journey—the opportunity of resting at full length within it.

Under this bulkhead Napoleon's camp bedstead still reposes, neatly encased within a receptacle some six inches square and three feet long, folded, ready to be withdrawn at a moment's notice. When and where this bedstead was last required for its master's use are points of interest often conjectured, but as yet not satisfied.

' Placed beyond the bulkhead, unusually forward
and high above the fore-wheels, is perched the
coachman's dicky—a dicky on which the coachman
must have sat alone, for its size excludes any
chance of companionship. It is supported by
slender scroll iron stays in a manner so mobile, so
sensitive to the slightest movement, that the poor
jehu who piloted the coach through those long
and weary journeys we know it to have traversed
must at times have felt sorely tempted to guide
his horses from their prescribed course and to steer
them away into the " Land of Nod."

The doors possess the simple distinction of
opening in the opposite direction from those of an
ordinary English carriage, whilst the Imperial
arms—a device borrowed of the Cæsars—are still
to be clearly deciphered upon both panels.

The ponderous under-carriage might well suggest
to the mind of a mechanic an instance in which
weight had far outbidden advantage in strength.
The heavy, split, crane-neck perch, the deep solid
axle-bed, and the cumbersome fore-carriage have
been constructed throughout in wrought iron,
and afford a good example of the coachsmith's work
of a century ago. The great cee springs are
in keeping with the rest, heavy and strong.
The thick leather straps plying them, and
carrying the full weight of the body of the
carriage and all contained within it, are
still in sound condition and quite capable

of doing their work ; but by way of precaution they have now been relieved of all strain, and the weight is borne by four iron standards springing directly from the floor.

The wheels, even compared with others of the period in which they were made, are very heavily dished. Following the Continental manner, the spokes are arranged in pairs, so that their spacing out might be described as two close together and two wide apart—those placed near together entering the rim near where the felloes join, presumably with the object of adding strength at a weak point.

The rims are made up of seven felloes fixed together with iron clamps. The iron tyres, heavy and rough, are secured to the rims with bolts and nuts, instead of, as in our day, by rivets and burrs. The hubs, or stocks, large and massive, are further strengthened by stock hoops, the flange on the outer hoops of the fore-wheels being hexagonal, while those on the hind-wheels are of a plain round shape.

The axles are curiously primitive—simple nut-axles used from time immemorial—the wheels being held in position by means of strong rough iron nuts screwed on at the extremity of the axle arms and further secured by a pin passed through a hole at the end of them. Strangely enough, the axle-ends are absolutely devoid of caps.

Behind on the foot-stage, or rumble, there still

rests, as on the day the vehicle was taken, the odd-looking and spacious shoe-shaped trunk in which so many articles of apparel belonging to Napoleon were found. This is doubtless the source from which have flowed during the past century not a few genuine, but also numberless doubtful, belongings attributed to the great Napoleon which have been offered for sale under the " incontestable " sworn testimony of so many irresponsible and illusive authorities as having been found in Napoleon's carriage captured at Waterloo.

The four black square metal lamps fixed in a rough-and-ready way with iron rods to the corners of the coach have a simple and quaint appearance, but otherwise have little about them to call for comment. They have been made to take large wax candles, and have the usual spring sockets to hold them.

CHAPTER XV

THE interior of the carriage is even more interesting than the exterior. Glancing within, we immediately find ourselves in closer touch with things personal to the great Emperor.

We find therein provision for a couple of passengers only. Here are two deep and roomy seats, divided by a tall movable arm-rest, offering the occupants unusual freedom and comfort. Confronting these seats, set high up on the front of the vehicle, are a pair of windows affording each traveller a full view of the driver and of the road and country beyond. Beneath these are displayed those objects of interest which have so readily engrossed the attention of many millions of visitors who, during the century past, have been moved to inspect the carriage.

Opposite to that seat usually occupied by Napoleon—that is to say, the one on the offside, following our rule of the road—there hangs a brass

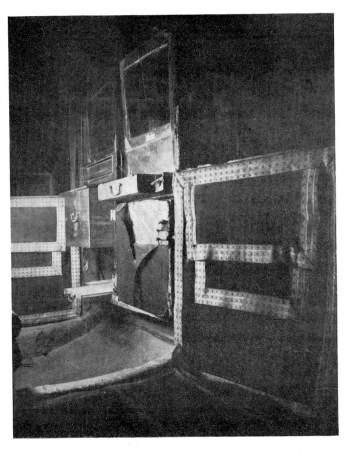

NAPOLEON'S MILITARY CARRIAGE.
(ii.) The Interior.

[To face p. 94.

handle which is apparently attached merely to a simple shallow drawer. An easy pull at this reveals a strong and well-appointed writing-desk, capable of being withdrawn far out of its recess. This action, with the aid of a writing-slope that unfolds from the top, enables the desk to span the space between the front of the carriage and the seat, thus giving to its occupant all the facility and convenience desirable for carrying on a correspondence at leisure.

Nor is this the only accommodation the desk provides. Some time after the carriage had changed ownership it was found that an extra pull withdrew the desk still farther from its aperture, and upon this being done a secret compartment was discovered behind it, in which were found jewels and money of great value.

On the right side of this desk, fitted into a narrow but deep recess, there rests a long, wedge-shaped box made to hold a goodly supply of those quills of which Napoleon was so uncommonly prodigal.

Below these fittings, and readily engaging attention, is a large cloth-covered door, hinged to open towards the middle of the carriage, so that when butting against the arm-rest of the seat it divides the lower portion of the interior into two separate parts. When so placed it exposes a large cavity constituting the lower part or foot of a sleeping compartment, the seat of the coach serving for the head, and the space between being bridged by a plank or board. In this cavity were found all the necessary things for making up a complete and comfortable bed.

On the near side of the front interior, placed immediately under the window, is a shallow rack made to take small things such as sealing-wax, wafers, paper-knife, etc., the receptacle being furnished with a wooden flap and catch to enclose it. Underneath this is a large and strongly made drawer that pulls out endways. In it many things were discovered which were in immediate use before the capture of the coach, among them several pieces of a silver service containing articles of food remaining from a meal.

Below this again there is an opening, which has never boasted of a door to enclose it. At the bottom of it a brass-bound rest, or table, has been fitted between grooves so that it may be drawn out, or pushed in, as occasion required. This also forms a bridge to unite the recess with the seat facing it, so as to provide a second sleeping compartment when found necessary.

On the inside of the doors hang heavy cloth lapels covering large square pockets, edged with broad gold-coloured gimp braid speckled with blue spots. On the outer side of each seat is a deep hole, both of which contained a loaded pistol ready at hand in case of emergency.

Well above and running across the back of the seats is a half-circle recess serving as a gun-rack, forming a strange protrusion viewed from the outside of the coach.

An oil lamp, which at best could have yielded but a feeble light, takes up the customary position in the centre at the back of the carriage.

The interior is lined throughout with a dark-blue cloth, in colour and texture similar to that used at the present day for the same purpose.

A fairly reliable inventory of things found in the carriage on the night it was captured has been handed down to us, and the following is a copy :

A beautifully constructed and marvellously well-appointed *nécessaire*, comprising some seventy pieces, a few in solid gold and many mounted in the same metal (a present from Marie Louise to Napoleon on the eve of his departure for the Russian campaign of 1812, and designed and carried out under her immediate supervision).

Several parts of a solid silver service, engraved with the Imperial arms.

A large silver chronometer.

A green velvet cap.

A mahogany liquor case, containing two leather-covered bottles, one filled with rum and the other holding a small quantity of sweet wine.

A pair of spurs.

Two fine merino mattresses.

An assortment of the finest bed and other linen.

Many toilet requisites, among them a cake of Windsor soap.

A steel camp bedstead, still in position on the carriage, in the case made to hold it under the boot.

A uniform, sword, and cocked hat.

A rich and costly Imperial robe.

A handsome diamond head-dress, or tiara.

A pair of pistols, loaded, found in recesses at side of seats.

H

Many gold medals with Napoleon's portrait and name engraved upon them.

An article devoid of intrinsic value, but nevertheless possessing an exceptional interest—namely, a musket-ball flattened out to the shape of a thin medal, found carefully put by in the secret drawer at the back of the desk; a missile, maybe, that ended the days of a friend, or one possibly that endangered Napoleon's own life.

A considerable number of mounted and unmounted diamonds found secreted in various parts of the carriage, three hundred of these stones alone being discovered in the above-mentioned *nécessaire*.

The jewels and other articles easy of acquisition fell, for the most part, to the lot of Major von Keller's men of the 15th Prussian Infantry Regiment of the Line, which was that night under the command of General Count Gneisenau.

The coach was drawn by a team of six of the finest brown Normandy horses, four driven by the coachman, the leaders under the control of a postilion.

When the coach was overtaken by the Prussians —that is to say, about a quarter-past eleven at night, outside the town of Jenappe—the postilion and the leaders were killed outright, whilst the coachman, severely wounded, was left for dead upon the road. Recovering from his many wounds —one of which entailed the loss of his right arm— he was induced by Major von Keller himself to come over to this country with the coach and horses. These were exhibited, as a very special attraction for the Christmas holidays of 1815, at

NAPOLEON'S MILITARY CARRIAGE.
(iii.) Scene of its capture at Jenappe.

the London Museum (then but recently opened by Mr. Bullock) in Piccadilly, a house of entertainment that was soon to be known to future generations as the Egyptian Hall.

And now for a century has this old war-coach been held up for the inspection of the passer-by, and, in its turn, has been the dumb witness of many a fleeting and touching episode. For as it stood have not time and men passed on ? Has it not beheld many a young gallant, with the honours of the campaign fresh upon him, recounting to wife and child the story of that last great battle that closed the Empire of the first Napoleon ; many a veteran son of Mars telling his grown sons how that great day was won ; many a kindly warrior gently helping his children's children to mount the steps and learn how on that day old " Boney " was made to fly, and nearly got caught in the act ?

But those to whom the old coach must have brought back so many vivid memories of that famous victory, and who had the greatest right to enter it, have themselves moved on ; and now its doors have been fastened up and the old chariot encased for secure keeping, not indeed against the ravages of time, but, with regret it must be said, safe away from the hands of those who would not scruple to despoil it.

CHAPTER XVI

The St. Helena carriage—Napoleon alarms the ladies—Certificates of authenticity.

THIS is the last carriage in which Napoleon is known to have ridden.

On his first arrival at St. Helena he took much exercise in the saddle, but during and after the year 1818, until he ceased venturing beyond the precincts of Longwood, he made constant use of this vehicle.

The following extract from Mr. Norwood Young's very valuable contribution to our Napoleonic literature, *Napoleon in Exile at St. Helena*, gives us an insight to the manner in which it was used :

> After the dictation and the reading, Napoleon, in the afternoon, generally went for a drive, one of the ladies, with Bertrand or Las Cases, being taken in the carriage. The two Archambauds at first used six horses, afterwards reduced to four, which they drove, as postilions, at a great pace. The round of the wood, done at high speed, was soon covered, and the course would then be repeated. Madame de Montholon declared that they went so fast that it was difficult to breathe. At this rate the wood was so often driven round that, in spite of the excitement of dodging the trees, there came a staleness in the sport. In the

early days the outing would be varied by a visit to the
Bertrands at Hutt's Gate, and all the ladies became much
alarmed as the vehicle dashed round the corners, with
the terrible precipice on one side.   It was indeed dangerous,
for there were no barriers, and a little carelessness might
have sent the whole party down the abyss.   There is now
in most places a low earth bank, a railing made of gas-pipes,
and a plantation of flax at the edge, which at least conceals
the danger.

When the Bertrands had moved from Hutt's Gate the
drives never went beyond the Longwood estate, which
has a circuit of about four miles.

Who built the carriage and how it came to be
transported to St. Helena, we know not.   In type
it is what was then—and for the matter of that
is still—known as a " barouche."

Yellow and green are the prevailing colours in
which the body has been enamelled, the former
predominating to a considerable extent.

Ponderously built throughout, as indeed were all
travelling carriages of this period, the body is
swung so that its full weight is cast upon the
hind-wheels.

The under-carriage is strong and cumbersome,
like that of the Waterloo carriage, standing by
its side.   Its heavy cee springs are overlaid by
strong leather straps upon which the body is
comfortably slung.   The carriage is lined throughout
with heavy green superfine cloth.

So far as its general appearance is concerned,
it might well be designated as unexceptional.   It
has no mark or devices upon it to indicate that it

constituted the equipage of a royal household, and the axle-caps have not even the maker's name upon them.

The following quotations from an old Catalogue published at the time when the conveyance was first installed in our collection of Napoleonic relics remove any doubt as to its authenticity:

237. CARRIAGE used by the Emperor Napoleon, during six years of his exile at St. Helena, and the last he ever entered. Certified by the Counts Montholon and Las Cases. The following is the letter, with description, from Mr. Blofeld, of whom it was purchased:

"DEAR SIR,

"In accordance with your request I send you the following brief particulars of the carriage used by the Emperor Napoleon at St. Helena. I purchased it in 1848, at that island, of Major Charles Sampson, an officer who had lived highly respected there for more than fifty years, and who gave me the following certificate:

"'Received from Mr. John Blofeld, for Bonaparte's old carriage, the first used by him on the Island of St. Helena. (Here follows the amount paid.)—(MAJOR) C. SAMPSON.'

"In 1850 I went to Paris, where I showed it to General Count Montholon and Count Emanuel de las Cases; those gentlemen immediately recognised it, and both said they had frequently rode in it with the Emperor, and they most kindly gave me the following certificates, which, as you purchased the carriage, I enclose. General Montholon informed me that the Emperor always used it, drawn by four horses, ridden by two postilions, with the head of the carriage down.

"Certificates:

"'I hereby certify that the carriage shown to me at Paris by Mr. John Blofeld is the actual carriage used by the Emperor Napoleon at the Island of St. Helena.—(GENERAL) MONTHOLON.'

" ' I hereby certify that the carriage shown to me by Mr. John Blofeld, and purchased by him of Major C. Sampson, of St. Helena, is the actual carriage used by the Emperor Napoleon at that island.—EMANUEL DE LAS CASES.'

"   I remain, Dear Sirs,
"   Yours faithfully,
"   JOHN BLOFELD.

" Messrs. Joseph and Francis Tussaud,
"   London, Jan. 8, 1851."

CHAPTER XVII

ONE of the greatest of all temperance reformers was Father Mathew, " the Noble Priest of Cork," who persuaded sixty thousand people in London alone to become teetotallers and to take a pledge to that effect. The apostle of temperance was induced to come to London in the early forties to give a series of lectures.

Some were delivered at Hall's Riding School (now a motor garage) in Albany Street, opposite Holy Trinity Church and close to Great Portland Street Station, and Mr. Francis Tussaud (grand-father of the writer) modelled him in one of the rooms of that place. He was constantly interrupted during the sittings by people of all classes and creeds coming in to take the pledge. Most of them insisted upon kneeling to receive Father Mathew's blessing. They were probably actuated by respect for him, and also by the hope that the recollection of his blessing might strengthen their teetotal vows.

At the close of the sittings Father Mathew

detached from his breast his temperance medal, which was attached to a ribbon round his neck, and handed it to the artist that it might be placed upon his model.

Father Mathew bore so striking a resemblance in face and figure to Napoleon I. that the two were once oddly mistaken for each other by our own servants.

We had occasion to renovate the portraits of the soldier and the preacher.   To do so it was necessary that the heads of both should be detached.   The assistant who was responsible for taking the figures to pieces in this way mistook the one head for the other.   The error was fortunately soon detected by Mr. Francis Tussaud, who had modelled both the heads, and he soon had the mistake rectified.

There are persons still living who remember Father Mathew.   An old and respected neighbour, Francis Draper by name, is one of the youngest men of eighty-seven one could possibly meet. Although born in 1832, he still possesses a wonderfully clear memory.

In 1842, when Father Mathew paid his visit to London, Mr. Draper—then a boy of ten years—was introduced to him at the Riding School.   In an anteroom upstairs, to which Father Mathew retired between the times when he administered the pledge, he saw an artist modelling his face in clay, which he was told was for Madame Tussaud's Exhibition.   He had an impression at the time that the artist was Francis, a son of Madame Tussaud, and his surmise was accurate, for it was Mr. Francis Tussaud who was executing the model.

For many years afterwards he saw " The Noble Priest of Cork " standing in a group in Madame Tussaud's, with his medal suspended round his neck, and, he says, it was the best likeness of anyone in the rooms.

The assassination of Alexander II. of Russia in March, 1881, recalls a quaint story of Voltaire's chair, which stands in a corner of one of the Napoleon Rooms, not far removed from a collection of heads of leaders of the French Revolution.

This chair is one of our most treasured relics. It was made to Voltaire's own design, and is unlike any other chair we have ever seen.

After the *Entente Cordiale* between France and England in the forties, the visit to Queen Victoria of Louis Philippe was promptly followed by the arrival in London, in 1844, of Alexander's father, Nicholas I. of Russia, who, during his stay, was conducted over the Exhibition by Madame Tussaud's elder son, Joseph.

In the course of his tour round the galleries the Tsar's attention was arrested by the great Frenchman's wonderful chair. Being struck by its ingenious construction, he examined it very closely, and then, as so many persons have done, gave himself the pleasure of occupying the seat in which the famous satirist had spent many an industrious hour.

VOLTAIRE'S CHAIR.

[To face p. 106.

The chair was intended by Voltaire to facilitate his literary work, and, evidently taking account of his incessant labours, he had the arms extended without supports so that he could sit in any attitude and facing any direction, while a movable writing-slope was attached to be always within his reach.

So keen an interest did the Tsar take in the chair that we decided to make a replica and send it to him as a pleasant surprise. This was done, but no direct acknowledgment of the chair's delivery was ever received.

Months afterwards, however, two cases—one containing a splendid gallery portrait of Nicholas and the other a beautiful statuette of the same monarch—arrived at the Exhibition. These presents were accepted as a recognition, in practical form, of the chair. They could not have signified an Imperial bid for a place in the Exhibition, for a most lifelike model of His Majesty was already there.

Nearly forty years later, on the assassination of Nicholas's son, Alexander—to which allusion has been made—there appeared in one of our leading English illustrated papers, which gave pages to the story of the assassination, a full double-page picture of the Imperial study at St. Petersburg, and, behold, therein stood the identical chair which we had sent to Nicholas I.

It is interesting to note that on Wednesday, the 20th of October, thirty-six years later, a number of Princesses came to the Exhibition ; and among them was Princess Alix of Hesse, then a happy young girl of eight, and now mourned as the late Tsarina, who, as reported, shared with the Tsar and his family a terrible death at the hands of diabolical assassins during the recent Russian Revolution. Among the royal party which came on that day were our own Princesses Louise, Victoria, and Maud of Wales.

A great Wesleyan preacher and lecturer in his day was the Rev. Peter McKenzie, who died in November, 1895. He deserves a place in these memoirs on account of his characteristic and rather eccentric behaviour when he visited the Exhibition. In the course of his perambulation through the galleries he, like most of our patrons, found his way to the Napoleon Rooms, where Voltaire's chair immediately arrested his attention.

Striking an indignant attitude in front of it, the Wesleyan preacher exclaimed, "And this belonged to the man that was going to pull down the edifice of Christianity and sweep the religion of Jesus Christ from the earth!" So saying, he planted himself in the chair and, with a triumphant wave of his hand, declaimed to the wondering visitors gathered round the following verse of a well-known hymn :

> Jesus shall reign where'er the sun
> Doth his successive journeys run ;
> His kingdom stretch from shore to shore,
> Till moons shall wax and wane no more.

NAPOLEON'S BAROUCHE.

CHAPTER XVIII

ABOUT the year 1845 the celebrated Count d'Orsay, being, as usual, in a desperate state of impecuniosity, was absolutely afraid to venture out of Gore House (where now stands the Royal Albert Hall), except on Sunday, for fear of being arrested and imprisoned for debt.

It so happened that a portrait of one of the members of the Royal Family, painted by the Count, was just then in process of engraving, and it was necessary before the proofs could be struck off that d'Orsay himself should see and correct the work of the engraver. To do this the Count would be obliged to go to the engraver's house, and that gentleman, being of a devout and Sabbatarian turn of mind, utterly refused to receive d'Orsay on Sunday.

Finding himself in this difficulty, the Count asked the advice of his friend, Sir Edwin Landseer.

"I should risk going on a weekday, if I were you," said Sir Edwin. "Wrap yourself up carefully, come and have breakfast with me in St. John's

Wood Road, and then we will go together to the engraver."

This they accordingly did, and, greatly to Landseer's relief, the Count passed through the streets unrecognised.

Not content, however, with escaping thus far, d'Orsay found his freedom so delightful that he became reckless, and did not seem at all disposed to return in any haste to his captivity.

" It is so long since I have seen London on any day but Sunday, I will enjoy myself now," said he. " Can't we go to some place of amusement together ? "

Landseer suggested Madame Tussaud's, an Exhibition which d'Orsay had never before seen ; and to Baker Street they went. The Count, charmed with the novelty of the wax figures, was childishly delighted with all he saw, until a moment when he became conscious that his footsteps were being dogged by two suspicious-looking individuals.

" Do you see those men ? " said d'Orsay. " They never take their eyes from me."

" Yes, I see them," answered Landseer, who had really noticed them for some time, but thought it wiser not to say anything on the subject to his friend. " Let us go into the Chamber of Horrors."

Accordingly they paid their extra sixpences and entered the mysterious inner room. The two men followed them. Landseer gave up his friend for lost. After a few moments of suspense one of the two men advanced towards d'Orsay, hat in hand, and, making an elaborate bow, said :

" Have I the honour of speaking to M. le Comte d'Orsay ? "

No escape seemed possible now, so the Count drew himself up and answered with much dignity :

" Sir, I am he."

" Then, if M. le Comte will be so very kind as to allow me, Madame Tussaud presents her compliments, and she will be greatly honoured if M. le Comte will give her some sittings and will permit us to add his illustrious figure to those already in our establishment."

Finding that all his anxieties were at an end, d'Orsay forgot his dignity in a moment, almost embracing the man in his sudden joy, and exclaiming, with his accents of broken English :

" My dear fellow, you shall do what you like."

The handsome face and distinguished figure of the Count were, of course, sufficiently remarkable to attract attention anywhere, and Madame Tussaud had too keen an eye for business ever to let slip so excellent an opportunity.

This may be regarded as an interesting reminiscence of the old rooms in Baker Street and the people who used to frequent them three-quarters of a century ago.

Although we know that Queen Victoria came

to visit the Exhibition in Baker Street as Princess Victoria, there is no direct evidence that she ever came as Queen.

There is, however, a story that on one occasion Her Majesty paid a private visit with her children. When it is remembered that the Cattle Show used to be held in the rooms underneath the Exhibition, and that Her Majesty used to pay it at least one annual visit in those days, it is quite reasonable to suppose that the Queen would take an opportunity of going upstairs.

The story goes that seventy years ago, a fortnight after an auctioneer had murdered Mr. Jermy, Recorder of Norwich, and his family, at Stanfield Hall, near Wymondham, a Norfolk farmer came to London for the Cattle Show, and was an unconscious interviewer of Queen Victoria in the Exhibition.

I will give the narrative in his own words, being unable to vouch for its authenticity.

" After," said the farmer, " I had been to the show and carefully examined the different animals, and given my meed of praise to the breeders and their feeders, I thought I would devote a spare hour to Madame Tussaud's celebrated Exhibition. Accordingly I presented myself at the door, and paid my money.

" On entering, I was surprised to find that I was the only spectator. Undisturbed for some time, I wandered about, looking with astonishment

at the waxen effigies, habited in their gorgeous
apparel.

"In a few minutes some ladies and children
arrived, and, standing near to one of the former
I said, 'What ugly, grim-looking people some of
those kings and queens are!' The lady smiled
and answered, 'I perfectly agree with you; they
are!'

"My attention was soon arrested by hearing
one of the party, pointing to a figure, mention
Lord Nelson, when, proud of having been born
in the same county as the illustrious sailor, I could
not help exclaiming, 'Ah, he was from my neighbourhood!' Upon which one of the ladies, advancing
said to me, 'Then you are from Norfolk? Pray
can you tell me anything about poor Mrs. Jermy
with whose melancholy fate I so deeply sympathise?
Have you any information different from that
which has appeared in the public papers?'

"To this I replied, 'No, madam, for I have
been some days from home.'

"Scarcely had this conversation ended when
Madame Tussaud herself entered, and seeing me
there asked me how I got in, and if I did not know
she had forbidden the entrance of anyone. I
replied I did not; but, having paid my money
had walked in as a matter of course.

"Judge of my surprise when she informed me
I had had the honour of speaking to no other than
our good and gracious Queen, and that the lady

I

whose tender anxiety had been so warmly expressed for the injured widow of Stanfield Hall was the same illustrious person whose exalted rank does not, however, so elevate her but that the misfortunes and afflictions of others can reach her heart and excite her generous commiseration.

" The party who accompanied Her Majesty were the royal children and their attendants."

CHAPTER XIX

WELLINGTON gazing upon the effigy of Napoleon is one of the many instances of a really fine picture being produced from an original work executed in our studios. Upon it hangs an interesting story.

Early one morning, soon after the Exhibition had been opened for the day, Joseph, Madame Tussaud's son, who had been wandering through the rooms, as was his habit, perceived an elderly gentleman in front of the tableau representing the lying-in-state of Napoleon I.

The model of the dead exile rested—as it does down to this very day—on the camp bedstead used by Napoleon at St. Helena, and was dressed in the favourite green uniform, the cloak worn at Marengo (bequeathed by Napoleon to his son) lying across the feet. In the hands, crossed upon the chest, was a crucifix. In those days it was the custom to lower at night the curtains that enclosed the bed, in order to exclude the dust, whereas now the whole scene is encased in glass.

Observing that the visitor was desirous of seeing the effigy, and no attendant being at hand, Joseph Tussaud raised the hangings, whereupon the visitor removed his hat, and, to his great surprise, Joseph saw that he was face to face with none other than the great Duke of Wellington himself.

There stood his Grace, contemplating with feelings of mixed emotions the strange and suggestive scene before him.

On the camp bed lay the mere presentment of the man who, seven-and-thirty years before, had given him so much trouble to subdue.

No feeling of triumph passed through the conqueror's mind as he looked upon the poor waxen image, too true in its aspect of death ; he rather thought upon the vanity of earthly triumphs, of the levelling hand of time, and of how soon he, like his great contemporary, might be stretched upon his own bier.

Mr. Joseph Tussaud used frequently to recall this dramatic meeting between the Iron Duke and the effigy of his erstwhile foe, and to imagine the feelings of the old General as he gazed upon the couch. It was probably the first of the Duke's many visits to the Exhibition.

A few days after this most interesting visit Mr. Tussaud, who was an old friend of Sir George Hayter, related the incident to that artist.

WELLINGTON VISITING THE EFFIGY OF NAPOLEON.

(From the picture by Sir George Hayter.)

Hayter was immediately struck with the potential value of the event for the production of a painting of the historic scene, and the Tussaud brothers at once commissioned him to execute the work for them.

Sir George thereupon communicated the idea to the Duke, who readily responded, and offered to give the necessary sittings. We have the sketches made by Hayter in preparation for the work, and among them appears a drawing of Joseph Tussaud himself, although he does not enter the actual picture.

Hearing that the artist was making progress with the painting, the Duke visited his studio, and, having expressed himself warmly in appreciation of the picture (the figures had been but lightly limned in at the time), said :

" Well, I suppose you'll want me to sit for my picture here ? "

Hayter has given us a most characteristic portrait of Wellington as he then appeared. He is dressed in his usual blue frock-coat, white trousers, and white cravat, fastened with the familiar steel buckle. He stoops a little as was his wont, his head is lightly covered with snow-white hair, and his manly features are marked with an expression of mingled curiosity and sadness as, hat in hand, he looks upon the recumbent Napoleon. The picture was completed early in December, 1852, and has been on view in the Napoleon Rooms at the Exhibition ever since.

The engravings of the picture have been circulated in thousands throughout the world, and, strange to say, they are exceedingly popular in Austria. It is an interesting fact that the painting in question was the last portrait for which the Duke ever sat.

This story brings to mind several instances in which the members of the Tussaud family, especially in days gone by, have produced subjects for other artists to paint from. For example, the model of Marat stabbed in his bath—which has been shown in our Exhibition ever since it existed in Paris —was modelled expressly to assist the famous David to paint his picture representing the death of the miscreant.

Strange to say, a replica of this painting was offered to us a year or so ago, and the dealer who submitted it insisted that it was the picture from which our model was copied. He looked woefully incredulous when it was explained to him that the boot was on the other foot, and that the picture had been copied from the model.

On one occasion, in a newsagent's shop, a lady customer asked for a picture postcard of King Edward. Several were shown to her, but after inspecting them she pushed all the direct photographs on one side, and selected the print of a figure that had been modelled. The shopkeeper subsequently stated that this card was almost invariably chosen in preference to others.

In recent years there has grown a curious disposition on the part of certain publishers to exploit for their own purposes work produced in our studios. This is not to be wondered at when photographs of our models have been so often mistaken for portraits taken direct from life.

We have ourselves on many occasions photographed our likenesses for reproduction by the Press ; and, apart from this, newspaper representatives, times out of number, have requested permission to take a photograph ·of figures in the Exhibition for the use of their own journal.

There is also the inevitable snapshotter, who neither asks permission nor cares whether it is granted or not.   Such individuals seize an opportunity when few persons are about and take an illicit " negative " without risking a verbal one.   The result has been that the photographs thus secured— all subject to copyright fees never collected—have been made use of for all kinds of purposes ; they have turned up as blocks in newspapers and magazines, illustrations in books, and portrait postcards, besides being treasured in albums and framed as pictures.

Only very occasionally has a statement accompanied publication acknowledging the source from which the picture has originated—a circumstance that has more than once led to a curious and, so far as the artist is concerned, a somewhat vexatious contretemps.

It has so happened that we have had sometimes to send a member of our staff in quest of all the latest photographs of a favourite celebrity whose figure we have desired to remodel and bring up to date. Not infrequently has he brought back with him " photographs " purporting to have been taken from life, but which have been instantly recognised as reproductions of figures in the Exhibition.

A droll incident once occurred illustrative of this strange situation.

Many years ago, when Mr. Joseph Tussaud, under pressure of time and with very meagre material to go upon, produced a portrait of the late Pope Leo XIII. directly after he was elevated to the papal chair, a certain well-known firm of photographers were at their wits' end to obtain a portrait of the new Pontiff, and the novel idea suggested itself to them of arranging to borrow for a short time Madame Tussaud's model, and therefrom obtain an original negative that might fulfil their requirements. This they accordingly did, and the object was achieved with remarkable success, for the portrait challenged detection. So lifelike was the picture that when it was placed upon the market beholders concluded that the Pope had sat for it.

Another firm of photographers, some time afterwards, and at great trouble and expense, succeeded in obtaining sittings from the Pope himself.

When the portrait taken from life appeared, and

was compared with the photographs from the model, very grave doubt was raised as to whether the new portrait was really a good likeness, and many persons questioned its genuineness, much to the chagrin of the photographers who produced it.

CHAPTER XX

An ephemeral celebrity of a bygone day, who fittingly comes into the picture at the present time—for we are still dealing with events that happened in the seventies—was Colour-Sergeant Gilbert H. Bates, of the 24th Massachusetts (U.S. Artillery) Regiment.

This gallant soldier of the Federal Army, after carrying the Star-spangled Banner through the Southern States of America to prove that the war had not killed the respect felt for the national flag, crossed the Atlantic, in fulfilment of a wager, and bore the Stars and Stripes from Gretna Green to London, amid most enthusiastic scenes, demonstrating that Bates was right when he insisted that John Bull and Uncle Sam were the best of friends at heart.

Mr. Joseph Tussaud modelled a portrait of the sergeant, who had an honoured place in the Exhibition for several years.

Bates was a patriotic American who had a firm

belief in the friendship of the English people for their American brethren.

For 1,500 miles through States whose streets had been stained with the blood of civil carnage he had marched with the national flag to the strains of patriotic music, an eloquent tribute to his country-men's deep-rooted love of peace. His passage was a triumphant success, and the exploit is handed down to posterity in Captain Mayne Reid's stirring poem " From Vicksburg to the Sea," the first of its five verses being :

> Bear on the banner, soldier bold !
>   How Southern hearts must thrill
> To see the flag, so loved of all,
>   Waving above them still !
> What chords 'twill touch, what echoes wake,
>   Of that far truer time !
> Who knows but it the spell may break
>   That maddened them to crime.

This was remotely the origin of Bates's English expedition. Calumny was rife in the States. No theme had been so often discussed for the two years then past as that of the feeling of John Bull towards Uncle Sam. The malicious craft of certain politicians had led them to foster elements of hatred towards the Old Country, and a corrupt section of the Press had lent itself to the unworthy task of exaggerating trifles and distorting facts to suit the fancies of gullible readers.

It was in the course of one such discussion as to the feeling of the English towards Americans that

this lover of concord was led to make a wager of
100 dollars against 1,000 dollars that the people of
England would not insult the flag of America, but
would welcome it heartily wherever it should be
borne by an American soldier. Not a few of his
compatriots were incredulous of his success, and
they predicted that he would miserably fail ; while
one said, " I bet he don't travel twelve miles before
he sets face homeward and leaves his bean-pole in
the custody of some parish beadle."

The gallant sergeant was determined and confident,
however, and, taking passage in the Anchor liner
Europa, he crossed the Atlantic.

Bates was a small but well-built man, 5 feet 7½
inches in height, square-shouldered and square-
headed, clean shaven, with clear grey eyes, dark
hair, and swarthy skin. His age was thirty-four,
and he wore the uniform of a sergeant of the Federal
Army. He is described as modest, intelligent,
well-informed, and a very good specimen of the
unassuming, matter-of-fact, and practical Yankee.

. The flag he carried was from a piece of army
bunting from the headquarters of General Sheridan.
It was of regulation size, 6 feet by 6½ feet, and the
hickory staff measured 9 feet. Before he left he was
assured by a Member of Parliament in Chicago that
as the Americans had honoured the English Prince
when he visited that country, the English people, in
return, would honour the American " prince "—
which was their flag. And so it turned out.

On the 5th of November, 1872—Guy Fawkes Day and the anniversary of the Battle of Inkerman—Sergeant Bates left Edinburgh for Gretna Green, that romantic spot at the southern extremity of Scotland. It was with difficulty that he managed to leave the northern city without unfurling the flag, as his Scottish friends felt that they should have an opportunity of testifying their good feelings to the banner which waved over so many of their kindred in homes beyond the Atlantic.   But his mission had been planned, and he had decided to begin his march from the border of England itself.

With no quiver of fear and with a heart full of gladness, he stood upon Sark Bridge and, uncovering his head, gave the Star-spangled Banner to the breeze. A few merry rustics greeted him with cheers, and the historic march was begun. The country before him was England, the mother-country, the home of the English language, the freest and most peaceful country in Europe.

He reached Carlisle that evening without anything more important happening than a rigid cross-examination by an excited old woman as to whether he was heralding a Fenian invasion, and an anxious inquiry from a little boy as to when the circus would arrive.

At the Bush Hotel at Carlisle a party of commercial travellers gave him a right hearty British welcome, and this henceforth became the order of the day at whatever town or village he put in an appearance. News of his coming preceded him, and his progress was one continuous ovation, culminating in a veritable furore when he reached his journey's end.

Through Penrith and Shap, where he was cheered by the miners, who had sent men from the quarries to watch for his approach, he made his way to Kendal, where, at a dinner given in his honour, he announced that he had written to cancel the wager he had made. He did this in token of the purity of his motives, and to prove that he was not actuated by mercenary considerations.

From Kendal he proceeded to Lancaster, which city he entered followed by an enormous crowd, a similar concourse escorting him to the outskirts on his departure.

Garstang, between Lancaster and Preston, at that time enjoyed the peculiar distinction of having a Mayor and capital burgesses without its having been constituted a borough. Here he was entertained at a sumptuous repast, and the streets were full of people, the church scholars, drawn up in line, cheering the flag and its bearer as they passed.

The streets of Preston were lined with spectators ; at Chorley cheers were given for the Queen and President Grant ; and at Bolton the flag-bearer was presented with a pair of clogs, and given a live turtle-dove to take back with him to the American President.

He was almost carried by an eager, applauding

crowd along Bradshawgate on his way to
Manchester, and the *Bolton Evening News* of the
14th of November, 1872, records that "there was
more handshaking than we have ever seen bestowed
on any person. Far from insult, every respect was
shown to the flag of the great Republic, and," the
newspaper facetiously adds, " if the bearer is
rewarded all along his journey as he was at
Farnworth, his pockets will be filled with the metal
that makes the mare to go."

CHAPTER XXI

Sergeant Bates's journey finishes in London amid a remarkable
demonstration—His gift to Madame Tussaud's.

IN this chapter we conclude the story of the gallant
sergeant's historic march with the American flag
from Gretna Green to London.

At Bolton he was presented with a piece of silver-
plate, and a pedestrian gave him a pocket-knife;
but this gift was followed immediately afterwards by
a letter in which the writer said that as the giving
of a sharp instrument was regarded as a bad omen
and portended to cut friendship, he asked Sergeant
Bates to forward a penny stamp in the enclosed
envelope in order that the knife might be *sold* and not
given. The penny stamp was sent.

Five miles from Cottonopolis Bates was met by a
man who had been a lieutenant in the 24th Massachusetts Volunteers during the Civil War, who took
off his hat and said, "God bless our flag." Manchester
was reached on the 14th of November, and here the
flag had an immense reception, the crowd in Market
Street being so dense that the open carriage which
the sergeant was obliged to enter could scarcely make
headway.

128

Lodged at the Royal Hotel, he was presented with a Union Jack, and was pestered by several enterprising showmen, one of whom offered him as much as £60 a night for five weeks if he would only consent to lend himself and the flag ; but this he resolutely declined to do.

From Manchester to Macclesfield he met with a repetition of the same hearty ovations. The crowd kept slapping him on the shoulders, shaking hands, slipping money into his pockets, hurrahing, singing, and even dancing with joy before the glorious old flag.

At Macclesfield he was treated like a prince, royally entertained, and presented with a gold breast-pin by the Mayor. Through Congleton, Burslem, Stafford, Wolverhampton, and so on to Birmingham, the march was like that of a triumphant warrior, the crowds at Bates's heels, marshalled in military order, tramping along singing the national melodies of the two countries, " Rule Britannia " and " Yankee Doodle " being the favourite airs.

At West Bromwich, where the flag-bearer stood for a moment to salute the Union Jack, a man rushed out and crowned his flagstaff with laurel. He entered Birmingham escorted by a crowd of all classes, of both sexes and all ages, and the proprietor of the "Hen and Chickens" Hotel placed the house, the wine-cellar, and even his cash-drawer at his guest's disposal.

K

The crowd from Birmingham followed him for some miles out of the town.   There was a vast amount of handshaking, and several women insisted on embracing him, one old lady hugging him so unmercifully that she, he, and the flag were nearly sent sprawling in the mud.

One workman, bareheaded and without his coat, headed the procession in a perfect frenzy of excitement, and shook hands with Bates about every five minutes.   It appeared that he had served on the *Alabama*, and seemed to think that he was atoning for past transgression and ridding himself of the stigma of having fought against the Union.

Warwick was visited, and the castle inspected. The sergeant was shown over Shakespeare's birthplace at Stratford-on-Avon by a Mrs. Hathaway and a lady aptly quoted to him the line :

Still in thy right hand carry gentle peace.

At Leamington he was presented with an address and a silver Maltese Cross.   Southam and Banbury were passed through, and then he came to Oxford, where, it had been predicted, his mission would fail ignominiously.

But he was met by students from New College, who treated him with great gentlemanliness, one observing :

" Sergeant, you surely never expected that the people of England would fall upon one man, did you ? "

" No," replied Bates, drawing himself up. " I have come through England not only believing that my flag would not be insulted, but feeling sure that Englishmen would show it such respect everywhere that my countrymen would hail my coming as a step full of joyful hope for the future."

" Bravo ! " exclaimed the undergraduate.

Invitations poured in upon the happy soldier. He supped in University College and breakfasted in Trinity.

At a levee in the reception-room at the "Roebuck" the toast was given, " May the stars never shine with less lustre, nor the bars ever grow shorter," which was received with musical honours :

> It's a way they have in the Army,
> It's a way they have in the Navy,
> It's a way we have in the 'Varsity
> To drive dull care away.

On through High Wycombe and Uxbridge passed the soldier with his flag, and the crowd was great as he set out for Shepherd's Bush, whence he was to proceed through London.

There were incidents humorous and pathetic.

At one place an aged woman tottered up to him from a wayside house and, leaning on her stick, said :

" Let me touch the flag and give my blessing to the bearer. My youngest boy fought for that flag and died for it in your country. He fell with that flag in his hand."

Her son, an Englishman, had given his life fighting for the Union.

At another place a grimy sweep, fresh from a job, embraced the American most affectionately.

Bates's quarters at Shepherd's Bush were at the " Telegraph," and during the Friday evening the hotel was in a state of siege. Sir John Bennett, an ex-Sheriff of the City of London, had offered to lend the soldier a carriage ; but it was ultimately decided to use an open equipage drawn by a pair of greys, one of them mounted by a postilion.

The daily papers of the 2nd of December, 1872, give a full account of the proceedings. Seated in the carriage was Sergeant Bates, holding his beloved flag, while two other flags, the Union Jack and the Star-spangled Banner, trailed behind, the horses' trappings being decorated with international symbols.

Up Notting Hill, along Bayswater Road, and through Oxford Street passed the carriage, surrounded and followed by a huge and demonstrative crowd.

In Bond Street the horses were taken out, and the carriage was dragged by some twenty-five persons along St. James's Street, Pall Mall, by Charing Cross, and through the Strand and Fleet Street, up Ludgate Hill, and along Cheapside, to the Guildhall.

A dense mass of people had congregated in the Guildhall yard, where a British sergeant was carrying the English standard. The scene beggared description. The Guildhall itself was full to overflowing, and having alighted, Bates had perforce to be lifted on shoulders and hoisted, flag and all, back into the carriage, from which place of vantage he made a speech before refurling his banner.

He was delighted with his reception in the heart of the great Metropolis, and never forgot the sea of faces, the endless crowds, the fluttering flags, the waving handkerchiefs, the cheers, and the kindly greeting of that memorable day. His hand seemed to have been wrung into pulp, and he was struck with the phrasing of the oft-repeated salutation, " Give us your hand, old pal."

Cabmen had little American flags mounted on their vehicles or pinned to their horses' heads, ladies had the Stars and Stripes for carriage-aprons, and children waved toy flags.

Sergeant Bates was somewhat annoyed by relic hunters, who, could they have had their way, would soon have whittled his flagstaff into imperceptible pieces and riven the banner into a thousand shreds.

He gave a piece of flag and his boots to Madame Tussaud's Exhibition as a small offering to those of the British public " who," as he quaintly remarked, " worship such things, and who find at Madame Tussaud's perhaps the best field for the satisfaction of their curiosity."

Writing from the Langham Hotel, where he was staying, he observed that Madame Tussaud's had previously voted him a niche among the immortal heroes who adorned their Exhibition, a mark of honour for which he was told he ought to feel no small pride.

And what had Sergeant Bates accomplished? He claimed to have succeeded in bringing the two great nations' hearts near to each other, till they seemed to beat in unison, and the pulsation of the one was for a while that of the other.

"God grant," he said, "that work so begun may not willingly be laid down."

Although he was called at one and the same time "a hare-brained visionary," "a patriot," "a fool," "a man of courage," and "a remarkably shrewd, thoughtful individual," there can be no doubt that he did at least something to promote international amity, and to cement the feeling of warm friendship which was found to exist in this country towards her daughter America.

The continuation of that tie has been, and is still being, abundantly manifested ever since the United States joined the Allies in their recent determined fight for freedom; and there are thousands who echo Sergeant Bates's words:

"May the flags of both countries ever wave in freedom and peace till that 'far truer time' when there shall be but one flag, becausebut one people on the face of the earth!"

COLOUR-SERGEANT GILBERT H. BATES

of the 24th Massachusetts (U.S. Artillery) Regiment, who
carried the American Flag from Gretna Green to London in
November, 1872.

[To face p. 134.

CHAPTER XXII

My first model—Beaconsfield's curl—Gladstone's collar—
John Bright and the Chinaman.

WE now come to a period when I may well speak of
my own personal knowledge concerning men and
events in association with Madame Tussaud's
Exhibition.

The year 1872 was remarkable for several note-
worthy events. Two or three, in addition to the
National Thanksgiving Day for the recovery of the
Prince of Wales from serious illness, vividly recur
to memory. Among them was the assassination
of the Earl of Mayo, Viceroy of India, who was
stabbed by a convict while inspecting the settle-
ment at Port Blair on the Andaman Islands.

The models of the Prince of Wales and the murdered Viceroy were introduced to the Exhibition
within a few days of each other, and the sympathetic
public responded in great numbers.

A startling and remarkable tribute to the Viceroy's
portrait was " unconsciously " paid when the Earl's
housekeeper fainted on suddenly finding herself in
the presence of the model of her late master.

The first portrait I was entrusted with, as my father's understudy, was that of Prince Milan of Serbia, the memory of whom has long since passed into oblivion, like that of many others whose stay has been brief among the figures.   This was followed by a head of perennial interest, that of Benjamin Disraeli, which I was called upon to remodel on several occasions in after years.   Clearly do I recall his characteristic features, so marvellously grasped by Tenniel, whose cartoons in *Punch* I never tired of studying.

It will be remembered that one of the marked peculiarities of Disraeli's general appearance was the famous curl he wore upon his forehead.   Of that circumstance I am at this moment somewhat forcibly reminded by a letter disclosing the remarkable fact that the curl is still in existence, almost forty years after the great statesman has passed away. Here is an extract from the letter offering the forelock to us as a relic :

> Obersley,
> Near Droitwich, Worcester,
> March 7, 1918.
> My aunt, Miss Louise Hennet, nursed Lord Beaconsfield during his last illness, and the two locks (one the celebrated curl) were given to her. She was sent to nurse him from the nursing institution of St. John the Divine. The hair is enclosed in paper, which is endorsed in Miss Hennet's writing, and this can be identified.

The letter is duly signed.

It may be easily understood that the modelling

of the features of celebrated people stamps the memory of the artist with a deep and abiding impression.   I had but shortly seen my father produce a very striking portrait of Marshal Bazaine, solely remembered now for his dramatic surrender at Metz on the 27th of October, 1870.

A small knot of interested people attracted my attention towards a stout, elderly man of military bearing as he was leaving Mr. Adams-Acton's studios in Salisbury Place, Regent's Park.   I was astonished to recognise in him the living counterpart of the before-mentioned model.

It was Marshal Bazaine himself, who had but recently escaped from the fortress of Ile Ste. Marguerite, near Cannes.   I was much struck by the fact that the ill-starred soldier of the Second Empire looked in no way dejected, despite the disaster that had befallen his reputation.

I am often asked what are the qualifications people must possess for a place in Madame Tussaud's.   I can give no better answer than that the public shall demand to see them, for should the portraits of such people be omitted they are invariably inquired for by disappointed visitors.

It is astonishing how great a hold must be taken of the public mind by candidates for inclusion in Madame Tussaud's Exhibition before their election to our house would be welcomed by our patrons.

Of course, we are now associating our minds only with reputable society.   As regards the Chamber of

Horrors—of which I shall have something to say when the time comes—I may here remark that it is the notorious characters solely who seem to have a prescriptive right to enter that abode of gloom, which used to be called in the old days the " Dead Room," hardly so telling a title as the " Chamber of Horrors," for which, by the way, we are indebted to our dear old friend " Mr. Punch."

As to those people who retain a permanent place in the Exhibition, I suppose the secret is that, either by the example of their lives or through the medium of their works, they have deeply touched the heart or stirred the imagination of the people.

I suppose the British public never looked on two such political gladiators as Beaconsfield and Gladstone, and while these two statesmen dominated people's minds it was natural that they should both have a pedestal at Madame Tussaud's. I can neither say who was first to appear in the Exhibition, nor prophesy who will be the last to go. They are both there now, and still attract much notice from persons of all shades of political opinion.

So often had these figures to be remodelled, to keep pace with the changes worked by time and the strenuous nature of their public service, that there must now repose, carefully stowed away in our " catacombs," impressions of their features sufficient to cover the whole gamut of their political careers.

For more than a generation the Beaconsfield curl and the Gladstone collar exercised a subtle influence in the political world, mainly through the cartoons and caricatures of John Tenniel and Harry Furniss.

One has to be meticulously careful with regard to important details such as these ; and when Mr. Gladstone's figure had to be remodelled in later years, it was thought advisable, in order to be quite correct, that a collar actually belonging to the " G.O.M." should be inspected.

Mr. Gladstone was living at Carlton House Terrace at the time the new portrait was in progress ; and our " Master of the Robes," who was responsible for the accuracy of detail respecting all Exhibition costumes, called there, and, on examining the statesman's collars, was surprised to find that they were of quite normal size, and not so high as the caricaturist represented them to be.

As a matter of fact, the collars were made to fit loosely round the neck, and thus allowed the wearer's chin to sink behind their upstanding ends. It is gratifying to record that permission to view her husband's collars was graciously given to our representative by Mrs. Gladstone herself.

On a certain occasion when Mr. Gladstone had been notified that Mr. Harry Furniss, the originator of the big collar, would be at a dinner to which he himself was invited, the Liberal leader purposely wore a collar of more than usually modest dimensions, possibly as a gentle rebuke to his caricaturist.

The model which approached nearest to these in popularity at the time was that of John Bright, the great Anti-Corn Law Leaguer and apostle of Free Trade.   His portrait has long since stood beside that of Richard Cobden, and these two inseparable reformers must remain together for good, as they laboured together in their lives.

It was on one of the occasions when Bright's likeness had been brought up to date that an incident, rather flattering to the modeller, occurred in the House of Commons.

An influential Chinaman, on being shown the sights of London, was taken to the Houses of Parliament, where he happened to notice a prominent member passing through one of the lobbies.   Without ceremony the Chinaman pounced upon John Bright, and shook him heartily by the hand.   The genial statesman was highly amused at the spontaneous greeting, and inquired how it was the Chinaman knew him.

" Oh," he replied, " I knew you at once.   I have just come from seeing you at Madame Tussaud's."

CHAPTER XXIII

The Tichborne " Claimant "—Nearly an explosion—The big
man's clothes—The real heir—The Claimant's release
from prison—Confession and death.

I CAN hardly allow this period to pass without making
some reference to the fact that from 1872 till 1874—
when he was sentenced, on the 28th of February, to
fourteen years' penal servitude—the name of the
" Claimant " to the Tichborne baronetcy and estates
was on every lip, and it seems to me that no trial
in my time has ever engrossed public attention to
such a degree.

People flocked to see the Claimant's portrait when
it was added to the collection, and perhaps that was
the first time one saw queues assembled outside the
doors of Madame Tussaud's.

The various incidents of this historic case absorbed
my youthful attention, and I recall how, at his house
in Kentish Town, the Claimant submitted to the
ordeal of having an impression taken of his hands
to show the curly thumbs and a scar on his wrist
which formed subjects of comment in the courts.

I was struck by the Claimant's enormous size,

which yet did not seem to hinder his movements, for the agility of the bulky man was indeed extra-ordinary ; and equally surprising were the acuteness of his mind and the suavity of his manner.

To save him the inconvenience of fulfilling appointments in the Exhibition studios, my father had a special gas-light fixed at the Claimant's house that sittings might be taken in the evenings.

This device, curiously enough, once put the life of the Claimant in jeopardy. An old gasfitter in our employment, named Dallender, who had done some stage work, introduced an apparatus such as was used in the theatres. Something went wrong with the manipulation of the arrangements, and the room became charged with gas. A servant was about to enter the apartment with a light, when the Claimant himself stopped her on noticing the strong smell. But for this fact the famous Tichborne trial might have had a sudden and tragic termination.

The Claimant showed certain qualities which hardly tallied with the character of the " uneducated butcher " he was declared to be. Proof that he had some refinement of feeling—or was he merely actuated by that vanity frequently found among men of his class?—may be inferred from an incident that greatly impressed my father.

The Claimant had promised that he would provide a fresh suit of clothes for his model in the Exhibition, and, in fulfilment of his promise, after the sentence had been passed upon him, he beckoned from the table at which he was seated in court to an attendant, and handed him the suit of clothes, saying :

" Please see to these being delivered at Madame Tussaud's, as they are expected there."

This fact strikes one as being remarkable, having regard to the anxiety of mind he must undoubtedly have suffered at the close of the trial.

It was a curious coincidence that I revisited my old college at Ramsgate about this time, and there had pointed out to me, among the students, the young heir to the Tichborne estates, whose title had been made clear by the conviction of the Claimant for perjury.

The students were on their way to the refectory, and the youthful heir appeared more concerned over the prospect of a good dinner than the result of the case upon which his future depended.

Stories of the Claimant were countless as he strode like a Colossus through the country in the long interval between his civil case and the criminal trial that succeeded it.

He was mobbed by sympathisers everywhere, and men and women shook hands with him, as if it bestowed a distinction on themselves. There was one amusing story at the time of a wealthy Yorkshire manufacturer whose wife said to him when they entertained the Claimant to dinner :

" John, how we are slithering into Society ! "

After he had served eleven years' imprisonment, his sentence having been reduced through good

conduct, the Claimant came to the Exhibition to learn
if he could be of any further service to us, or we to
him.   His ponderous bulk was so much reduced by
prison fare that we should not have known him.   He
said he was none the worse for the period of enforced
" banting," which reduced his weight without
injuring his health.

The Claimant gave me several sittings at this
time, and a new model was substituted for the old
one.   He spoke freely of his prison experiences, and
said :

" It was not easy to be philosophical when set to
tease oakum, but eventually I bowed to my fate
cheerfully enough.   It is some consolation to know
that thousands still believe in the justice of my claim
to the Tichborne estates."

Notwithstanding this, the Claimant published in
a Sunday newspaper his signed confession, which
he is said to have afterwards recanted.

He survived his liberation from prison fourteen
years, and, gradually sinking into poverty, died in
obscure lodgings in Marylebone, not far from the
Exhibition, on the 2nd of April, 1898.   The name
engraved on his coffin was " Sir Roger Charles
Doughty Tichborne," thus maintaining his claim
to the very last.

CHAPTER XXIV

In 1873 the nation was saddened by the death at Ilala of Dr. Livingstone, the great missionary-explorer, who, some time before, had disappeared in the trackless wastes of Central Africa while preaching the gospel to savages and making surveys of the great continent. The name of Livingstone will always be bracketed with that of H. M. Stanley, who, as the emissary of the *New York Herald*, " discovered " him.

When my father wrote to Stanley asking for a sitting, he replied that he was too heavily engaged at the time writing his book *How I Found Livingstone*, and he proposed that the artist should call and make a study of him at his desk. This he did, with the happy result that he produced a very striking portrait.

The story of Stanley's life is a romance in itself.

Born of poor parents at Denbigh, in Wales, about 1840, he at first bore the name of John Rowlands. When about fifteen years of age he worked his way

L   145

as a cabin boy to New Orleans, where he was employed by a merchant, named Stanley, whose name he assumed.

He served in the Confederate Army, contributed to several journals, and in the year 1867 began his connection with the *New York Herald*. As its special correspondent he accompanied Lord Napier's Abyssinian Expedition, and the first news of the fall of Magdala was conveyed to this country by his paper. He next went to Spain for the *Herald*, and he was in Madrid in October, 1869, when he received the peremptory telegram " Come to Paris on important business." He immediately complied, and there received from Mr. Bennett, junior, the laconic instruction and valediction, " Find Livingstone ! Good-night, and God be with you."

In January, 1871, Stanley reached Zanzibar, and two months later marched into the heart of Africa.

It was on the 10th of November that he " found " Livingstone at Ujiji. Well, indeed, as Stanley himself admitted, was he repaid for all the dangers he encountered on his journey when he grasped the hand of the grey-haired old missionary—aged by climate and exposure—whose whereabouts he had been sent to discover.

We placed in the Exhibition portrait models not only of Stanley, attired in a facsimile of the explorer's suit worn by him on the occasion of the historic meeting, but also one of Dr. Livingstone himself. Probably many more persons have gazed upon the figure of Livingstone in the Exhibition than ever paid a pilgrimage to see his final resting-place in Westminster Abbey.

Together with the model of Stanley was placed a figure of his boy, Kalulu, concerning whom the explorer wrote a book in 1873 (*My Kalulu*).

The death of Napoleon III. in the January of this year was associated with one of the most impressive tableaux in the long history of Madame Tussaud's. The Emperor was represented as lying in state, and I find myself still wondering as to the identity of a tall, stately lady, dressed in black and wearing a thick veil, who came to the Exhibition on several occasions, bringing a bunch of violets which she placed on the steps of the catafalque, after having obtained a vase containing water in which to put the flowers.

The son of the Emperor Louis Napoleon, the Prince Imperial, who was killed in the Zulu War, was made the subject of an equestrian memorial at Madame Tussaud's some years later. The tableau closely conformed with authentic details of the Prince's attempt to mount his horse and escape from the Zulu hordes, who pierced him with many assegais.

It had been suggested in the House of Commons that an effigy to his memory should be erected in the Abbey, in view of the fact that the young Bonaparte died in one of England's wars while serving under English officers. A reference in *Punch* to this proposal suggested that a much more suitable repository for a memorial would be Madame Tussaud's along with the other memorials of the Bonaparte period on view there.

COUNT LÉON.
Natural son of Napoleon Bonaparte.
(*A Portrait Study by John T. Tussaud*)

[To face p. 149.

CHAPTER XXV

ABOUT this time I met Count Léon, the natural son of Napoleon the Great. The Count was then nearing seventy years of age, and had taken refuge in this country after the great *débâcle* of 1870. He lived in modest lodgings at Camden Town, and to pay his way set about selling the last remaining relics of the Imperial Family he had in his possession.

In a diary I now have before me I find that my father visited him on the 31st of January, 1873, the Count having expressed a wish to show him the family heirlooms, with the view to their finding a permanent resting-place among the many Napoleonic memorials at Madame Tussaud's.

The Count offered him a fine miniature of Napoleon I.'s brother, Lucien; a terra-cotta bust of Napoleon's mother, " Madame Mère "; and a snuff-box left by Napoleon with Count Léon's mother. The box contained a portion of the snuff which the Emperor had been using. There was also a lock of hair belonging to Napoleon's son, the Duc de Reichstadt, known in high Imperial days as the King of Rome.

One or two of these relics were acquired for the Exhibition.

The Count bore a striking resemblance to the Emperor, except in two particulars : his figure was cast in a larger mould, and his eyes were hazel, whereas Napoleon's were blue-grey. Count Léon returned to France, leaving behind him in London his son Charles, for whom I obtained a position in a City warehouse, where he remained engaged for several years, being at no pains to disguise his identity. My readers will readily see that the name granted to his father by the Emperor was composed of the last four letters in " Napoleon," a whimsical touch of Imperial humour.

Count Léon finally settled at Pontoise, some twenty miles north-west of Paris, first at the Villa Davenport in the Rue l'Hermitage and afterwards in the Rue de Beaujon. This was his last stage. The room that he made his final refuge he adorned with four portraits of Napoleon, " my glorious father."

To what depths had the Emperor's son fallen! The old man's shirts were in rags ; he could not afford clean linen ; he had to forgo tobacco. He died on the 14th of April, 1881, and without pomp or ceremony his body was laid in a pauper's grave. His only memorial was a grassy mound and a little black wooden cross that soon rotted and fell to pieces.

On the 2nd of July, 1873, the Shah of Persia, accompanied by his numerous suite, visited Madame

Tussaud's, and was accorded a private view with some pomp and formality. His visit to the Exhibition was deemed of such importance that it gained the unusual distinction of a special reference in the *Court Circular*. Members of our Royal Household in considerable numbers attended in state, and formed an imposing assemblage. The public was excluded.

The domes of the building were specially darkened to give effect to the internal illuminations, which were very beautiful. None enjoyed the function more than the Shah himself, who laughed heartily as he pointed at models he was able to recognise, and several times turned from a figure to a person present, indicating by a gesture and a chuckle his pride at discerning the likeness. The merry monarch even went so far as to pose among the figures as a real, live royal model.

Before leaving the Exhibition the Shah called for pen and paper, and, surrounded by the distinguished company, wrote in Persian the following : " Whilst staying in London I visited Madame Tussaud's Exhibition, and wrote these words here by way of memorial to my visit.—NASSERDIN CHAH KADJAR, 1290 Haegira (1873)."

The above free translation was there and then made by one of His Solar Highness's secretaries, and it possesses the charm of its own defects.

The " king of kings " was in his most humorously autocratic vein among the unhallowed figures of the Chamber of Horrors. He seemed to gloat over the collection of criminals and notorieties, examining with unaffected delight the guillotine which cut off so many heads during the French Revolution.

The lunette in which the necks of the victims were held in position greatly fascinated the Shah, who hinted that a condemned prisoner should be brought from one of the English gaols to be decapitated on the spot for the edification of himself and his attendants.

It was pointed out, as an evasive measure, that no condemned man was available at that moment, whereupon His Majesty turned to the members of his suite and called for volunteers.

Such a thing, however, as an execution at Madame Tussaud's was out of the question, even to gratify the whim of so illustrious a personage ; and the Shah's retainers looked genuinely relieved when they gathered that their royal master was not to have his way.

This period seemed to inaugurate a series of little wars, which, nevertheless, then excited the interest of the people, whose descendants may well remark how comparatively small these wars were. The Ashantee campaign ended in the fall of Coomassie on the 4th of February, 1874, and Sir Garnet Wolseley added fresh laurels to his fame. It was with real regret that the public looked in vain for the portrait of King Koffee at Madame Tussaud's. As the dusky potentate had evidently never had his photograph taken, and as "sittings" were out of the question, we could not very well gratify the public curiosity for lack of the necessary data.

Not only did people expect to discover King Koffee's portrait, but they also clamoured to see his famous umbrella, which Wolseley "borrowed" from His Majesty's mud-palace at Coomassie, and obviously failed to return, for the umbrella was accepted as a gift by Queen Victoria from the gallant Commander of this brief and brilliant expedition. We confessed then to a twinge of envy that the celebrated gamp had not found its way to Madame Tussaud's. We were, however, amply compensated by the public favour with which the portrait of Sir Garnet was received.

The deposed King of the Zulus, Cetewayo, who was subsequently restored to a portion of his kingdom, made a considerable stir when he visited this country as the "guest of the Government." A friend who was appointed to take shorthand notes when Cetewayo attended at the Foreign Office enabled me to gain a view of the burly black monarch, and I had an opportunity of comparing the original with the many published portraits.

He was a handsome type of a fine race, and looked a king even among the stalwart members of his suite, everyone of whom seemed to be six feet at least in height and well-proportioned.

Cetewayo's figure had been in the Exhibition some time before, and it now became possible to bring it up to date. Everything was done to impress Cetewayo with the strength of the British Empire ; but it was discovered that the objects which appealed most to his savage taste were the cattle in the fields, the cloth in the factories, and the gewgaws and jewels in the shop windows.

" He is uglier than that," said an envoy of the Induna King, Gungunhana, critically scrutinising Cetewayo's figure, when he visited the Exhibition in June, 1891.

This native envoy rejoiced in the name of Huluhulu-Untato, his companion being Umfeti-Inteni. They thought the figures were really dead bodies which had been preserved from decay. When told that they were merely waxen images the Indunas expressed disappointment that the white man had not completed his work by putting breath into the bodies.

When Huluhulu came before the figure of Queen Victoria he saluted Her silent Majesty, and stood audibly worshipping her for a minute or two.

CHAPTER XXVI

THE year 1876—in which we find the Prince of Wales arriving at Calcutta, the commercial metropolis of India ; " Empress of India " added to the royal titles of Queen Victoria ; and Disraeli's elevation to the Upper House as Earl of Beaconsfield—gave us subjects that kept our studios extremely busy, and also brought a constant stream of visitors to the Exhibition.

The portrait of the Queen had now to be remodelled ; that of the Prince of Wales appeared in the garb of a big-game hunter ; and Disraeli's doffed its ordinary attire for the robes of a peer.

Following these " moving " events, we now come to a period when the country became apprehensively aware of ominous happenings in the Balkan States.

Russia declared war on Turkey in 1877, and forced a clear road to Constantinople. This threat to our Eastern Empire aroused the spirit of war, particularly in London, and " gentlemen of the pavement," as Bismarck styled the men in the street, gloried in the ultra-patriotic sentiment which obtained the name of " Jingo " ; while music-halls and taverns rang with the rousing chorus embodying that distinctive epithet :

> We don't want to fight,
>   But, by jingo, if we do,
> We've got the ships, we've got the men,
>   And we've got the money too.

Lord Beaconsfield's prompt demand that a halt should be called to hostilities, for the adjustment of differences between the belligerents, led to the Berlin Congress, and gave us an excellent opportunity of adding an imposing group of the European statesmen who framed the Berlin Treaty.

Yet, so mercurial is the public taste, and so pronounced is the love of the British race for anything that is amusingly abnormal, that I doubt whether ten people did not come to see the " Turnerelli wreath " for one who came to scan the features of these great peace-makers.

" What was the ' Turnerelli wreath ' ? " the present generation may ask. It was the pivot of a political comedy that set the whole nation laughing.

Edward Tracy Turnerelli, a sculptor's son, and himself a sculptor, instituted a penny subscription to present Lord Beaconsfield with a gold laurel wreath, which he called " The People's Tribute," in appreciation of his many services to the State and in commemoration of his great part in the deliberations of the Berlin Congress.

Fifty-two thousand workmen subscribed their pennies in vain, for Lord Beaconsfield courteously, but firmly, declined the gift, and it was left on Turnerelli's hands ; while he, of course, could hardly be expected to refund the copper contributions.

I am indebted to Mr. J. H. Bottomley, Conservative agent for Clapham, for a copy of the following interesting autograph letter from Lord Beaconsfield, expressing his satisfaction that the course he had adopted in declining to accept the wreath had met with the approval of many who had been induced to sanction the proposed gift :

> 10 Downing Street,
> Whitehall,
> August 11th, 1879.

DEAR SIR,

I have the honour to acknowledge your letter of the 9th inst.

It gives me much satisfaction to learn that the course I felt it my duty to take with respect to a certain pseudo-testimonial has met with the approval of many of those who, originally, by misleading representations, were induced to sanction a surreptitious gift.

I am gratified by the suggestion, which, on behalf of various Conservative associations, you put before me, that I should receive a National Address of confidence as a substitution for the rejected offering, but when I call to mind that the present policy of Her Majesty's Government, unchanged and unshaken, is precisely the same as that which, scarcely a year ago, received an unanimous and most honourable expression of approval from the

Conservative Association of this country, I hope I am not presumptuous if, without now troubling them for its renewed avowal, I still venture to count on the continued confidence, which, then, was so welcome and so cheering.

Faithfully yours,
BEACONSFIELD.

The postman who delivered this letter to Mr. Bottomley offered him all his savings (£19 5s.) for the letter.

Mr. Bottomley received in five days, in 1879, more than 3,000 pennies from the working men of Oldham, together with the personal signature of each contributor, and he holds Mr. Turnerelli's receipt for the £13 5s. he sent him for the tribute.

The wreath was offered to us, and purchased at its gold valuation.

I looked at it to-day, and renewed my admiration of its artistic design and remarkable beauty. Every leaf is of gold, and under each one is inscribed the name of a town where a committee collected the pennies. The " tie " bears the inscription " Tracy Turnerelli, chairman."

While London roared and cynics wrote satirical quips, the promoter of " The People's Tribute " took its rejection very much to heart. I have seen a cabinet-size photograph of the disappointed sculptor, taken immediately afterwards, showing him with head thrown back, resting on his left hand, in a theatrical posture of profound despair.

Before the Beaconsfield wreath made the name of

THE TURNERELLI WREATH.
" The People's Tribute," offered to and declined by Lord
Beaconsfield in 1879.

[To face p. 158.

Turnerelli a byword, the public-spirited sculptor, who had spent a long time in Russia, vehemently opposed the Crimean War, as did also Mr. John Bright. Turnerelli was received by Lord Aberdeen on the subject, and the Prime Minister was said to have been impressed by the sculptor's sincerity and the cogency of his arguments. He also saw Lord John Russell, then Foreign Secretary, Lord Clarendon, and Lord Palmerston. In one particular he was vindicated. He declared that Cronstadt was impregnable, and as the war went on this proved to be the case.

Turnerelli, unluckily for himself, thereafter entertained the chimerical idea of presenting the golden laurel chaplet to Lord Beaconsfield, estimating that the cost of each leaf would be about £5. He succeeded, at any rate, in convincing sceptical people that there were at least 52,000 Conservative working men in the country. The wreath was made by Messrs. Hunt and Roskell, who put it on exhibition at their rooms. It was also shown to the Prince of Wales and other members of the Royal Family before being exhibited at the Crystal Palace.

Turnerelli's own explanation of Lord Beaconsfield's refusal to accept the wreath was a curious one. He stated that a " high legal functionary " warned Lord Beaconsfield that the wreath was a typical " Imperial diadem " which could only be loyally offered to a sovereign, and that it would be an insult to the Crown if a subject were to accept such a gift.

This same legal authority, Turnerelli said, reminded him that the promoter of such a presentation
would have been consigned, in previous reigns, to
the Tower of London.

These warnings came too late for Turnerelli, who,
had he known about them sooner, might have
substituted an inoffensive golden inkstand or a pair
of golden candlesticks.   But the wreath was allowed
to go on to completion, to be put on exhibition, and
to be written about in a light and fleering spirit ;
while the statesman to whom it was to be presented
offered no remonstrance until the pennies of the
52,000 working men had been spent on it.

Flippant people suggested that the whole affair
was a "plant" on Turnerelli's part to win from
Lord Beaconsfield some honour or emolument ; but
those who knew Turnerelli well scouted this insinua-
tion, and attributed the whole proceeding to the
guileless sincerity of the man.

Had he never embarked upon the wreath project,
he might have preserved some reputation as a writer
of topical political verse and pamphlets.   The
wreath, however, may serve to preserve his memory
longer, as an episode in the life of the great Conservative statesman whom he artlessly, rather than
artfully, desired to honour.

In a curious last will and testament Turnerelli
said : " I leave the gold laurel wreath to the nation,
provided my generous friends the Conservatives will
help me to cover the hundred and fifty pounds or

thereabouts I have personally expended upon it."

To a Birmingham gentleman, with whom he had almost completed negotiations for the sale of the wreath for £245, he wrote : " By the advice of influential friends I have determined to let Madame Tussaud & Sons have the privilege of exhibiting the wreath." Turnerelli compensated the Birmingham would-be purchaser for alleged breach of contract.

Punch, of the 22nd of November, 1879, contained the following : " What the Wreath has come to.— The brows of Lord Beaconsfield at Madame Tussaud's. *Punch* said it would, and it has."

Funny Folks said: " The Beaconsfield Wreath is at Madame Tussaud's, probably worn by his lordship's effigy. Curious that this emblem of popularity should be on the wax, while the popularity itself is on the wane."

It may be stated that the gold wreath never rested on the waxen brows of Lord Beaconsfield, despite what *Punch* said to the contrary.

I am reminded that, in his latter days, Turnerelli sought consolation for worldly disdain in designing and constructing his own tombstone. This was erected in Leamington Cemetery about four years before his death, and serves as a monument not only for himself, but also for his father, who was a famous sculptor in the early part of the century, and is buried in London.

After the erection of the tombstone the younger
M

Turnerelli regularly went to gaze at it for an hour or two.   The block is surmounted by an imitation in stone of the famous rejected wreath.

Turnerelli died at Leamington on the 24th of January, 1896, aged eighty-four years.

EDWARD TRACY TURNERELLI.
Promoter of " The People's Tribute " refused by Lord
Beaconsfield.

[To face p. 162.

CHAPTER XXVII

The Phœnix Park murders—We secure the jaunting-car and
pony — Charles Bradlaugh — General Boulanger—Lord
Roberts inspects the model of himself.

THE requirements of the business have often necessitated our sending fairly far afield in quest of
exhibits, and this has seldom been done without
success, as people with desirable relics to dispose of
appear to have recognised the claims of Madame
Tussaud's.

Between seven and eight o'clock on Saturday
evening, the 6th of May, 1882, Lord Frederick
Cavendish, the newly appointed Chief Secretary for
Ireland, and Mr. Thomas Burke, the Permanent
Irish Under-Secretary, were stabbed to death in
Phœnix Park, Dublin, and twenty " Invincibles "
were subsequently tried for the murder, five being
hanged, three sentenced to penal servitude for life,
and nine to various terms of imprisonment.

James Carey, who turned Queen's evidence and
was acquitted, paid for the betrayal of his associates
with his life, for he was shot by Patrick O'Donnell
on board the *Melrose Castle*, near Port Elizabeth,
South Africa, on the 24th of July, 1883. The

Government, in their efforts to get Carey safely into another part of the world under an assumed name, were thus outwitted by the "Invincible" avengers.

It had been intimated to the management of the Exhibition that there was a chance of Madame Tussaud's obtaining from Michael Kavanagh the jaunting-car in which the assassins drove to and from the scene of the crime. Kavanagh was a typical Dublin jarvey, with an almost unintelligible brogue, from whom the car was hired. The assassins drove several miles circuitously about the scene of the tragedy with the object of escaping detection.

Our representative was forthwith sent to Dublin, and soon found himself in possession of Kavanagh's car. The good-humoured jarvey seemed glad to be rid of the vehicle ; anyhow, the price he asked was not a prohibitive one.

One thing was particularly noticeable, namely, that the number on the car differed from the number quoted in the newspaper accounts describing it when taken by the police. It was discovered, however, that the "Invincibles" had changed the number before the fateful journey. A condition was made by Kavanagh that the pony which drew the car should also be purchased, as he wished to have done with them both.

It took only a few hours to complete the transaction, and thereafter Kavanagh drove the purchaser over the ground traversed by the assassins in their endeavours to throw the police off the scent. This was a voluntary act on the part of Kavanagh, and our representative was curiously exercised at the time to understand why he imagined the trip should interest him.

To facilitate transit the car was taken to pieces by a coach-builder at Kingstown and wrapped in sacking, in the hope that it would not be observed. It was then put on the night boat for Holyhead.

The pony found a home in stables belonging to the Exhibition, and soon afterwards came to an untimely end from too little exercise and a too liberal allowance of provender. Why we did not sell the pony for what it might fetch is more than can be told to-day ; it may be surmised that such an expedient did not occur to our minds.

On the voyage across passengers whispered to each other that the Phœnix Park car was on board, and on its arrival in London there appeared among the latest telegrams in an evening paper : " Kavanagh's car goes to Madame Tussaud's." Evidently the Irish correspondents had wired the news of which we ourselves had hoped to make a special announcement.

The car was soon put together, and placed on view at the Exhibition in one of the rooms adjacent to the Chamber of Horrors, and in another part of the Exhibition were shown the portraits of Lord Frederick Cavendish and Mr. Burke.

After being exhibited many years the car was given to a gentleman who manifested an interest in it.

Its new owner had it renovated for his own use as a private conveyance, and he might often have been seen driving it in the streets of London, no one suspecting its notorious history.

Charles Bradlaugh sat many times to my father, and proved an entertaining and patient subject, sincerely desirous that his portrait should be a true representation of himself.   He discussed the troubles he was then passing through in the political arena over the oath, for which, after much contention, he was permitted to substitute an affirmation.

I remember him in his comings and goings, wearing a frock-coat and silk hat, tall and of commanding appearance, always affable and chatty.

A humorous writer of the day made fun of Mr. Bradlaugh's advent at Madame Tussaud's as follows :

> Tremendous excitement on the admission of Mr. Bradlaugh in wax into Madame Tussaud's establishment. Cobbett's figure gave an extra kick of delight, and as he offered his snuff-box to the unwelcome guest he assured him that he was a friend at a pinch. Oliver Cromwell, Cranmer, and Charles I. were indignant. The Russian giant is annoyed, and Tom Thumb threatens to make the place too hot for him. Figures waxing wrath !
>
> Latest telegram from Baker Street : " Bradlaugh cool ; great heat. Cromwell showing signs of melting ; all melting. Sleeping Beauty undisturbed."
>
> The latest latest : " Threatened with the guillotine in the Chamber of Horrors if they are not quiet. Tranquillity restored."

On many occasions it has been my office to accompany round the Exhibition visitors whose likenesses were at the time on view—always a trying ordeal.

I call to mind the visit paid by General Boulanger shortly after that meteoric ex-Minister of War quitted Paris for London to avoid arrest. It will be remembered that Boulanger was wounded in a duel with Floquet, his political antagonist, and that he dramatically ended his chequered life by shooting himself on the grave, in Brussels, of the woman to whom he was fondly attached.

As we stood before his facsimile, which had been only recently modelled, and, as it happened, represented him as considerably younger than his years, the General smiled and said, when I invited him to grant me a special sitting, " It is very, very good ; do not touch it." I fancied that, like most people, Boulanger had no objection to a flattering youthful reproduction of himself.

Boulanger's inclusion at Madame Tussaud's was the subject of a full-page cartoon by Tenniel in *Punch*, showing the be-medalled General standing in his stirrups on horseback and waving his hand as though in the act of delivering an important command. The cartoon was entitled " *Chez* Madame Tussaud's." An Exhibition employé was represented as saying to the little black-bonneted Madame—with a covert allusion to the General's political reverses—" Where is he to be put *now*, ma'am ? "

It was with a certain amount of surprise that I realised a short time ago, when the question was put to me by a prominent member of the Press, that during the thirty years I have been exclusively responsible for the modelling here, together with the fifteen or sixteen years in which I was working under my father, I must have produced, with studies, close upon a thousand models.

It is, of course, quite natural that many celebrities who pay a visit to the Exhibition, well knowing that their likenesses have a place within it, are not escorted round the galleries. For the most part, coyly and shyly they seek out their own models, and, more often than not, approach them with a concern born of a too-studied indifference that is sometimes extremely amusing.

" Bobs " was not of that order ; he was a notable exception to the general rule.

" Where's my figure ? " he asked plump and plain, and around it he stepped, quizzically examining it from various points of view. When he had satisfied himself that it was a fairly true representation, he ejaculated, " Not at all bad ! Not at all bad ! " and walked off to inspect the relics of the great Napoleon.

Lord Roberts's figure had been installed soon after his famous march from Kabul to Khandahar in the Afghan War.

CHAPTER XXVIII

OF all the portraits of my own modelling, I think, if I may be permitted to express an opinion, I like that of Lord Tennyson as well as any. It revives pleasant memories, and I will ask my readers if I may bring my wife into this part of my story. By a coincidence, as I raised my eyes at this moment, my glance fell upon a bust of Tennyson resting on a shelf in my studio.

About the time when I was engaged with the model of the great Victorian poet I had rented a farm cottage near Freshwater, Isle of Wight, and I remember my wife telling me that she frequently saw Tennyson in the neighbourhood.

On several occasions the poet, who lived at Farringford, near by, while taking his daily constitutional, came and leant upon the garden gate, evidently charmed with the beauty of the place. The old thatched roof and the quaint attractiveness of the cottage might well have given rise to reflections in less imaginative minds than that of a poet.

I had not the opportunity of studying Tennyson's features at that time ; but my wife, coyly hidden in a favourite spot in the garden, was able to observe him closely. Being herself an artist of no mean ability, she thus afforded me considerable help in the production of his portrait.

It seems strange that perhaps the most reclusive of men should have unwittingly come forward and posed, as it were, at the very door of the artist who was then desirous of obtaining sittings.

One day, while I was at work in the studio on Tennyson, I was visited by Father Haythorn-thwaite, rector of the Catholic Church at Freshwater. The priest was greatly interested, and he must have conveyed to the poet the intelligence that I was about to place his figure in Madame Tussaud's, for very shortly afterwards I learned that Tennyson was particularly desirous that I should bear in mind that, in spite of his four-score years, he had not a grey hair in his head—a touch of nature that seemed to me particularly human.

A nice but unintentional compliment was paid to one of our tableaux about this time by the present King, when he was Duke of York. We complied with a request to furnish a representation of the scene of the death of Nelson in the cockpit of the *Victory* for the Royal Naval Exhibition at Chelsea in May, 1891. This tableau was founded on the famous picture by Devis, which found a permanent home at Greenwich Hospital in 1825 ; and it was very well received by the visitors to the Exhibition. The compliment to which I allude was not heard by me, but it was reported in the Press at the time that the Duke of York, while looking at the tableau, exclaimed, " Why, this beats Tussaud's ! "

The tableau has been in our Exhibition ever since, and is a great favourite with all. When the present Prince of Wales and his brother Albert paid us a visit, the Sailor Prince looked long and intently at the historic scene. Both boys were also a good deal moved as they gazed on the tableau showing the murder of the two little princes in the Tower of London—a representation over which many impressionable people have been unable to keep dry eyes.

A great name with the past generation was that of Sir Richard Burton, who, sixty-six years ago, in fulfilment of a lifelong dream, made a pilgrimage to the shrine of the prophet Mahomet at Mecca when it was believed that no Christian could go there. Besides being a great explorer he was a man of scholarly attainments, and his translation of the *Arabian Nights* bears the stamp of an intimate familiarity with the Orient.

When Sir Richard died his remarkable career

became so much a subject of general comment in the Press that the British public awakened to the fact that a great Englishman had just passed away.

Apart from his literary achievements, the account of his exploits revealed so great a love of adventure and so much disregard for narrowing conventionalities as to leaven the story of his life with a very strong tincture of romance.

When modelling his figure I saw a great deal of his handsome and stately widow, and I am sure no woman could have taken a greater pleasure or more pains in assisting an artist with such an undertaking. Every thought, every action, she bestowed upon the work showed how deeply she cherished her husband's memory and how vividly the portrait stirred her imagination.

She clothed the model with perhaps the greatest personal treasure of his she possessed—that is to say, the actual garments her husband wore when he went on his famous pilgrimage to Mecca. She tarried long over the finishing touches that should make his presentment look its best before the critical eyes of the public should scan it. Ornaments, beads, trappings, had each her full consideration, and the very weapons of defence stuck anglewise in his belt were subjected to her most careful arrangement.

Of the capacity for taking pains there was no limit in Isabel Lady Burton's nature; but the labour in producing the figure, after many trying

SIR RICHARD BURTON.

Dressed in the clothes he wore on his
famous pilgrimage to Mecca.

(*Modelled by John T. Tussaud*)

[To face p. 172.

weeks, at last came to an end ; and there readily springs to my mind the pathetic picture of her bestowing upon the figure the few final touches, her fingers lingering over the pleats and folds of his robe ere she could declare herself satisfied that the task she had undertaken in helping with the model had been done at her very best.

There was one little difficulty, however, that she could not quite surmount. The costume was complete in every respect except one—the sandals he had worn on his hazardous journey to Mecca had become, owing to the wet and heat and the passage of time, mere tinder, and could not be placed upon the figure.

The following brief but interesting letter explains how this difficulty was overcome :

67, Baker Street,
Portman Square, W.,
May 22nd, 1894.

DEAR MR. TUSSAUD,

I sent you a pair of sandals yesterday belonging to me, but to-day I have had the promise of a pair from the Prior of the Franciscans which would suit much better. I shall send them directly I receive them.

Yours sincerely,
ISABEL BURTON.

The monument at Mortlake, on the Thames, within which now repose the remains of Sir Richard and his wife, consists of a white marble mausoleum, sculptured in the form of an Arab tent, its cost having been partly defrayed by public subscription.

CHAPTER XXIX

Removal of the Exhibition to the present building—Sleeping
"figures"—History of the Portman Rooms—The Cato
Street Conspiracy—Baron Grant's staircase.

AFTER fifty prosperous years at the old Baker Street
Rooms—now known as the Portman Rooms—it
became necessary that Madame Tussaud's should
find more commodious premises to meet the growing
popularity of the Exhibition.

The removal to the present well-known red
building was made in July, 1884, and the change
took about a week, during which the staff put in
very long hours. So strenuous a time was it that
some of them could hardly keep their eyes open
towards the end of this transition period.

There were considerably more than four hundred
figures, not to mention countless other things, to
transfer; and the models were cloaked for
conveyance, as the idea could not be entertained
of portraits of royalties, celebrities, and notorieties
being carried uncovered and exposed to the vulgar
gaze.

The wrapping of the images in sheets led to an
amusing incident after they had been removed.

174

Before they could be properly arranged and a fitting place assigned to each, the exhibits were placed in their coverings on the floor. This fact, it appeared, suggested to tired members of the staff a way by which they might be able to snatch a little rest.

Missing some of the men, my suspicions were directed to the prostrate exhibits, and I proceeded to prod the sheeted figures, with the result that here and there my attentions called forth manifestations of life. The weary helpers had laid themselves down to sleep among the models, hoping not to be disturbed. Although time was pressing, they were permitted to continue a few hours' well-earned rest with their pack-sheet cloaks around them.

Few of our visitors on the closing night were aware of the forthcoming change-over, and it was only when the band, after playing the last bar of the National Anthem, struck up " Auld Lang Syne " that the visitors realised what it all signified. There was a touch of pathos in the farewell scenes, and for the next week Madame Tussaud's Exhibition was not included among the sights of London.

When the old rooms in Baker Street were taken over for hospital uses in the war, my mind reverted to an historic coincidence of considerable military interest.

More than a hundred years ago what is now the Baker Street Carriage Bazaar formed the

barracks and stabling of the Royal Life Guards.
The place was then known as the King Street
Barracks. Old inhabitants of the neighbourhood
used to tell me that a regiment of the Guards
marched from these quarters on their way to the
field of Waterloo.

A little way off was the Portman Street Barracks,
from which Captain Fitzclarence set out to arrest
Arthur Thistlewood and his confederates in connection with the Cato Street Conspiracy—one of
the most desperate and foolhardy episodes in
modern English history.

Thistlewood and other members of the Spencean
Society—which might almost be described as the
prototype of latter-day Bolshevism—conceived the
mad idea that they could capture, among other
strongholds, the Bank of England, the Mansion
House, the Tower of London, and Coutts's Bank ;
but they found that the public sympathy on which
they counted did not exist. Thistlewood was
thrown into gaol for treasonable utterances, and
instead of imprisonment bringing him to his right
senses, he became more fanatical than ever.

The crowning act of infamy on the part of
this nineteenth-century " Guy Fawkes " and his
followers was to hatch a plot for the assassination
of Ministers at a Cabinet dinner in Lord Harrowby's
house, Grosvenor Square. The conspirators took
a loft over a stable in Cato Street, Marylebone,
where they accumulated arms, bombs, and

hand-grenades, vainly imagining that the police knew nothing of their movements, whereas the authorities were only waiting the right moment for action.

Thistlewood and his gang of desperadoes were arrested in the act of arming themselves for the wholesale assassination of the heads of the Government. In the scuffle Thistlewood killed a police-officer with his sword. The ringleader and four others, named Brunt, Davidson, Ings, and Tidd, were executed on the evidence of one of their own associates, who told the court that it was intended, in the first instance, to set fire to the King Street Barracks and either take the Life Guardsmen prisoners or kill them as they sat in their mess-room. This mess-room, fifteen years later, was occupied by Madame Tussaud's Exhibition.

Few, if any, of the thousands of persons who mount and descend the marble staircase which adorns the entrance-hall of Madame Tussaud's are aware that it originally formed part of a lordly pleasure house which was erected by the late Baron Grant on the site of what was one of the vilest slums (then known as " The Rookery ") in Kensington.

Who was Baron Grant?

The late Baron was born in Dublin in 1830. His real name, it appears, was Gottheimer. His parents were poor, and he had a hard upbringing. By dint, however, of industry, the sharpness of

N

his wits, and his great aptitude for business, he acquired wealth and a reputation in the City of London.

At the age of thirty-five he was elected M.P. for Kidderminster, standing as a Liberal-Conservative and defeating Lord Annaly, who was at that time a Lord of the Treasury. In 1868 he was appointed a Deputy-Lieutenant of the Tower Hamlets, and in the same year the King of Italy conferred upon him the hereditary dignity of Baron and appointed him a Commander of the Order of St. Maurice and Lazare.

These distinctions were well deserved by the then Mr. Grant for the services he had rendered in connection with the completion of the famous Victor Emmanuel Gallery in Milan, though in one of the burlesques of the period the decoration was scathingly referred to in the following couplet:

> Kings can titles give, but honour can't,
> So title without honour's but a *barren Grant*.

At the height of his prosperity Baron Grant built his princely mansion at Kensington Gore. It was never occupied, except for one night, when the " bachelors of London "—in other words, the smart young men of London Society—hired the house from the Baron's creditors and gave a ball of exceptional splendour.

The Baron was unable to pay the contractor,

and the mansion, known as "Grant's Folly," was pulled down because no one could afford to buy or rent it. The magnificent marble staircase, which cost £11,000, was bought by Madame Tussaud's for £1,000, and placed in our Exhibition.

The beautiful iron railings and gates of the " Folly " were purchased for the Sandown Park Club, where, I understand, they may still be seen.

Baron Grant was a keen collector of works of art, and once obtained the honour of being voted the thanks of the House of Commons for presenting a picture to the National Gallery.

It came about in this way.

On the 18th of May, 1874, a very valuable portrait of Sir Walter Scott was put up to auction at Christie's, and was eventually secured by Baron Grant for 800 guineas. The same evening Sir Stafford Northcote, the Leader of the House, was asked by a private member why the Government had not purchased so fine a work of art for the nation. He replied that the Treasury had no funds available for the outlay. Thereupon the Baron rose and stated that he had already written offering the picture to the Trustees of the National Gallery.

Sir Stafford immediately proposed a vote of thanks, and this was carried with much enthusiasm.

Eight hundred guineas, however, was far from being the largest sum which the Baron spent on a single picture. He gave £10,000 for Landseer's " Otter Hunt," and the value of his collection may be judged from the fact that it realised £106,000 when the inevitable crash came and his art treasures passed under the hammer to pay his creditors.

The great benefaction for which Baron Grant will always be remembered is the gift of Leicester Square to the Metropolis at a cost to him of upwards of £30,000. For years this Square had been dilapidated and a disgrace to London, with a huge hoarding round it. Baron Grant secured, by purchase, all the rights of the owners. He then planted the gardens, and erected in the centre the statue of Shakespeare by Signor Fontana. This was, at the time, the only statue of the world's greatest dramatist existing out of doors in his own country. The liberal donor also placed in the Square busts of celebrated men who had lived in the neighbourhood. These included Sir Isaac Newton, John Hunter, William Hogarth, and Sir Joshua Reynolds.

This act of munificence did not bring the Baron the popularity he so much desired, for after the princely gift was presented by him to the Metropolitan Board of Works on the 2nd of July, 1874, the following verses were freely sold at the opening ceremony :

Of course, you've heard the news that Baron Grant,
To gain what most he wants—a good repute,
Has promised to reclaim
Wild Leicester Square, so long the West End's shame,
And turn that waste ground, nigh Alhambra's towers,
Into a smiling garden full of flowers.

But will the world forget these flowers of Grant's
Are but the product of his City " plants " ?
And who, for shady walks, will give him praise
For wealth thus spent, *when gained in shady ways* ?
In short, what can he hope from this affair ?
Save to connect his name with one thing Square !

It was this same public-spirited though erratic
" plunger " in stocks and shares who, in February,
1875, widened, at his own cost, the road leading
to Kensington House, so as to avoid the curve
which was dangerous to carriages when driving in.
It was an approach that Queen Victoria frequently
used.

CHAPTER XXX

THE King of Siam and the Shahzada of Afghanistan are linked in my memory because of the peculiar interest King Chulalongkorn took in the Afghan Prince, whose model appeared in all the splendour of one of the Shahzada's own State dresses.

The moment the King of Siam was confronted by this portrait he exclaimed in surprise :

" How did the uniform come here ? Where did you get it ? "

" Oh," I replied, " we purchased it."

" Whom did you get it from ? " the King of Siam persisted. " From the Shahzada himself ? "

The information was imparted that the elaborate costume had been offered to us by a member of the Shahzada's suite, who took a keen personal interest in the transaction, and gave us to understand that his royal master would prefer that the portrait should not wear his own clothes till after his departure from this country.

We complied with this condition, and while

writing these reminiscences the gorgeous apparel of the Afghan Prince lies heaped in a corner of my studio, having been brought out that I may again for a moment gaze upon its faded glories of purple and gold; for the portrait of the Shahzada has long since been removed from its pedestal.

The King of Siam was a very decorous and unassuming little gentleman, who gave no hint of disappointment that his own portrait did not appear in the collection, while I wondered, as I walked with him, whether he regretted or welcomed the omission.

As we came face to face with the Shah of Persia, whose gorgeous habiliments glittered with a veritable firmament of jewels, the King again harped upon the question of the Shahzada's clothes.

Looking hard at the " lion " of a former season, the King exclaimed :

" His own clothes, too, I suppose ? "

" Not this time," I replied. " We were not so fortunate in the case of the Shah."

" An exact duplicate, though," was the compliment of the laughing King.

The Eastern potentate was a most minute and intelligent observer of all he saw, and questioned me unceasingly.

" Who is that beside the Prince ? " he inquired, pointing at the Prince of Wales in a howdah on the back of the elephant Juno, a tableau which

depicted a tiger-hunting incident in the late King
Edward's Indian tour.

On being told that the Prince was accompanied
by his " loader," the King replied, " Yes, yes," as
if he thought his question a superfluous one.

From hall to hall we passed, and I was astonished
at the knowledge of English history displayed by
King Chulalongkorn. He picked out the figure
of Richard I., and, pointing to the white doublet
with the red cross on the breast, said, " The costume
of a Crusader—certainly, certainly." The representation of King John with the Magna Charta in
his hand did not appear to produce a very pleasing
impression upon the Siamese autocrat.

" *What* a name ! Who was he ? " remarked the
King in front of Houqua, the big Chinaman who
earned his place in the Exhibition on account of
certain services he had rendered this country. I
had withdrawn for a moment, and was called back
to explain that Houqua was a Chinese merchant,
whereat the royal interlocutor turned away with
a contempt for trade clearly indicated on his
face.

It was surprising to note that King Chulalongkorn
passed the portraits of Mr. Gladstone, Lord Salisbury, and other British statesmen without a pause
or comment. He stood some minutes in front of
the case containing the orders of the Duke of
Wellington, and then remarked, with admiring
emphasis :

" These are surely all the orders a man could have ; he must have had nearly everything."

The group of Henry VIII. and his six wives was surveyed in stolid silence by a monarch not likely to be moved by such a spectacle. In a shadowed portion of the gallery he nearly mistook (and slightly frightened) two nice English girls in white for wax figures.

In the Chamber of Horrors he showed from his observations that he was familiar with the main features of several of the crimes commemorated there.

I may add that every honour was done the King on that occasion. We had the public excluded from the Exhibition, and the Siamese National Anthem was played on his arrival and departure.

The King of Siam's inspection of the elephant reminds me that, beside the stuffed monkey which one of the wives of Henry VIII. is fondling, the only animals ever shown in the Exhibition were in the " Tiger Hunt " scene in question. The tusker was the famous Juno, which was for many years the King of Burmah's war elephant.

The Prince of Wales had just mortally wounded a male tiger, and was about to give the *coup de grace* to another beast which, unexpectedly springing from the jungle, had been pinned to the ground by Juno. The animals were stuffed and staged by the late Mr. Rowland Ward.

When I say that these were the only animals shown in the Exhibition I mean, of course, dead ones.

Within the past twelve months a monkey that escaped from the Zoo, barely a mile away, entered the Exhibition by a back window, and was seen in the act by a crowd of people, who had been amused by its antics outside.

It appears that the monkey, in scurrying through the building, caught sight of its dead counterpart on the lap of Henry's Queen, and tried to attract its attention. Failing in this, the little creature pawed it, and the result was electrical.

The strangeness of coming unexpectedly in contact with a dead animal which was thought to be alive seems to have startled the monkey beyond measure, for it became terrified, and, springing away, went at great speed to the remotest part of the Exhibition, where it took refuge in one of the side rooms.

Several visitors, mostly ladies, were in the room at the time, and they at once made for the door, which was thereupon locked upon the animal. Meanwhile we had telephoned to the Zoo that one of the monkeys had escaped and was in the Exhibition.

A keeper arrived shortly afterwards, and said he had missed it from its cage. Both keeper and monkey were delighted at their reunion. The

monkey had not seemed to trouble much about
the figures, which it probably took for living people,
but the dead monkey on the lap of one of them
had been more than it could stand.

CHAPTER XXXI

IN the early part of 1898 we purchased from an
enterprising journalist four interesting copperplates
—three of them etched by Queen Victoria and one
by the Prince Consort. Of the four plates, three
were done by the Queen within a year of her
marriage.

Although not altogether faultless from an artistic
point of view, the work is most conscientiously
executed, showing how painstaking was the Queen
even in comparatively trivial matters.

After her marriage Her Majesty found in the
Prince Consort a fellow craftsman, and forthwith
a room in Buckingham Palace was fitted up as a
sort of combination studio and workshop. Here,
under the guidance and advice of Sir Edwin Landseer, assisted by Mr. Henry Graves, the fine art
publisher, the young couple worked for two or
three hours in the morning.

Nor would the Queen allow any portion of the

process to be performed by an assistant. Even the printing was done either by herself or her husband, a small press being set up for that especial purpose.

It is understood that portraits of the royal children thus reproduced are preserved in the print-room at Windsor Castle.

I have already described how the Shah of Persia (Nasr-ed-Din) paid a private visit to the Exhibition in the year 1873.

I must now relate the circumstances that attended the visit of his son, Muzafir-ed-Din, who came to this country for the coronation of King Edward in 1902, thirty years later.

The " Brother of the Sun " came on the 19th of August. He was attended by the Earl of Kintore and Sir Arthur Hardinge, and I received His Majesty, while the orchestra played the Persian National Anthem.

The first model he asked to see was that of his late father, but unfortunately his picturesque parent had disappeared to make room for more up-to-date people.

The horrible fact of the remelting to cast a possibly much less distinguished personage could not, of course, be divulged to the royal visitor. A hint to the entourage was sufficient. " *Perished by fire—great accidental fire,*" explained Sir Arthur Hardinge with the aplomb of a true diplomat.

" *Big fire*," echoed the sombre Persians sadly in their own tongue.

The Shah listened to a description of the models in French and made his comments in Persian, a course of procedure which was not helpful to those who would have liked to glean His Majesty's impressions.

By this time the news that the Shah was in the building had spread, and the people began to throng around him. It was difficult to say whether he appreciated the curiosity of the crowd or not. A merry little party of Japs beamed upon the dusky potentate from the Far East, and the two extremities of Asia thus metaphorically rubbed shoulders.

The tableau of " Queen Victoria at Home " pleased the Eastern sovereign most. He looked at it longest.

The scene depicting the Gordon Highlanders storming the Heights of Dargai also captivated him. The place where the battle was fought was not very remote from the borders of His Majesty's dominions, and he was, no doubt, familiar with the history of the wild tribesmen of the north-west frontier of India. He was an eager auditor while the Gay Gordons' feat was narrated in French and Persian.

Face to face with his own portrait model, the Shah addressed some presumably humorous remark to it, for sovereign and suite relaxed their facial muscles simultaneously, and a Persian outburst of mirth succeeded. *The stolid monarch actually laughed outright.* It was the only recorded laugh of His Majesty during his visit to this country.

But what did he say to that waxen presentment? The features of the model were certainly rather darker than those of the Shah, but the observation in Persian of the monarch was darker still—at any rate to me. Turning aside, he remarked, in French, that though the features were excellent, the complexion was not quite fair enough—a disclosure of an undoubted Eastern vanity.

He closely scrutinised the figures of reigning sovereigns, and on coming to that of the young Queen of Holland he exclaimed, in French, " Ah, I have seen Her Majesty." The Shah quickly noticed Mr. Balfour among the group of politicians, and gazed eagerly at the representation of the meeting between Lord Roberts and Cronje at Paardeberg.

Whether the Shah was made nervous through the proximity of the crowd, I cannot say, but he neglected to visit the Chamber of Horrors and the Napoleonic relics (which latter he had expressed a desire to see), and made a straight line for the exit before those who were chaperoning him realised the meaning of the movement.

The Chamber of Horrors would have been an attraction to at least one member of the suite.

This gentleman was fascinated by the group in the Hall of Tableaux representing the execution of Mary, Queen of Scots. He stood gazing with dilated eyes upon the scene, and had to be called on by a touch on the arm before he could be made to realise the unreality of the drama.

At an Exhibition supper at which " Viscount Hinton" was present, we having modelled his figure and purchased his organ on the death of the old Earl, to which title he now laid claim, a speaker, in proposing my health, began " Mr. Chairman, my Lord, Ladies and Gentlemen." That was enough for " Earl Poulett." He rose and bowed in recognition of the compliment paid to his degree, and when the speaker finished he made a speech in which he referred to a few incidents in his organ-grinding career.

He sat to me for his model, and we bought the suit of clothes he was wearing, although a friend of his told his " lordship " that he would not have picked them up from the gutter.

It appears that " Hinton " went to the Bank of England with the £50 note we gave him, and, as is customary, he was asked to sign his name. With a flourish he wrote down " Poulett," whereupon the cashier said, " Christian name as well, please." Hinton drew himself up and said, " We earls always sign our names like that," a remark which, doubtless, duly impressed and abashed the cashier.

In June, 1901, as the Exhibition was closing for the day, several pieces of jewellery, valued at between 50 and 60 guineas, were discovered to be missing from the figure of the Old Coquette, facing the model of the sardonic but courtier-like Voltaire, who is seen raising his hat to her. The gems had served to adorn the representation of this curious-looking old dame for a period of more than a century.

As soon as the discovery was made the usual notification was given to the police. Strange to say, while the detective-officer was in consultation with us discussing the most likely means of recovering the articles, a bulky envelope, bearing the mark of the Earl's Court postal district, was handed in containing the missing property, with the following short note enclosed: "Found at Madame Tussaud's—thrown down."

o

CHAPTER XXXII

MADAME TUSSAUD'S was one of the last places
visited by the King of Spain and Princess Ena
before they left this country for their wedding at
Madrid in May, 1906.

Somehow there seemed to be at the time an
atmosphere of anxiety attending the visit of this
vivacious royal couple, and I feel sure this uneasi-
ness was felt by many who observed them pass
freely and jocularly among the visitors, who were
very numerous that afternoon in the Exhibition
rooms. Disquieting rumours had reached this
country that an attempt would be made by certain
disaffected ruffians to interfere with their marriage.
Plots and threats of a sinister character were in
the air, and, as we all know, these culminated in a
crime of a particularly atrocious nature in the
Spanish capital.

Yet none seemed to be less affected by these
disturbing influences than the young royalties
themselves, while I am quite certain neither of
them was acting a part. They were simply as
happy as a bride and bridegroom ought to be who
were counting the days till they should be united.

The young King took a positive delight in moving among the visitors, and none was less self-conscious than he. I was amused to find him bubbling over with fun and frolic standing in front of his own portrait.

Then he did the thing one almost expected he would do. To the amusement of all beholders he exclaimed, " Let me shake hands with myself," suiting the action to the words, and laughing heartily with his bride and her friends. It is for traits like this that King Alphonso enjoys popularity wherever he goes.

The visit passed off happily, and I for one felt somewhat relieved when they had taken their departure without molestation, although I had no tangible reason to harbour the doubts that possessed me.

On returning to this country soon after the tragic accompaniments of their marriage, the light-hearted young King took an early opportunity of revisiting the Exhibition, and in passing gave a familiar nod of recognition at his own portrait, as one might salute an acquaintance in the street.

He roamed about the place in the least ostentatious way, and took a noticeably keen interest in the figure of the great Duke of Wellington, who, among his numerous foreign honours, received the titles of Duque de Ciudad Rodrigo and a Grandee of the first class, 1812—titles granted by predecessors of King Alphonso on the Spanish throne. As was the case with the King of Spain and his bride, members of the Royal Family on numerous occasions have paid their shillings and gone in " with the crowd," their object being to stroll round without having to undergo the worry of a " reception " and its attendant red baize and " blowing of trumpets."

Soon after his marriage with our then Princess Royal, the late Emperor Frederick of Germany, who was at that time Prince Frederick of Prussia, decided to pay us a visit. This was rather more than fifty years ago.

Hearing of his intention, my father decided to withdraw his figure, deeming it to be too youthful and out-of-date to bear a favourable comparison with its living counterpart—a severe test for even the best of portraits.

When the Prince arrived it appeared that he had come with the main object of inspecting his own model, for he had not been long in the place before he exclaimed, " Where is my figure ? "

This was a question that rather nonplussed the member of my family who had undertaken to cicerone His Royal Highness through the Exhibition.

There was nothing for it but to make the plain, straightforward admission that it had only just been removed, and to give the reason for this having been done.

Notwithstanding this, the Prince's request to view the portrait was reiterated, and he was so emphatic and persistent that there was nothing to be done but to replace the figure before his very eyes.

It was a strange proceeding, that of having to withdraw the model from the side room into which it had been removed, to march it through the spacious galleries with the Prince amusedly looking on the while, and ultimately to dump it down in his old place among the figures in our big royal group.

The Prince, with great good-humour, scanned it with a lenient eye, and pronounced it to be by no means a portrait of which anyone need be ashamed ; in fact, he appeared quite pleased with it, and when he left the Exhibition he seemed to be highly delighted with his unique and interesting experience.

Many years ago, in the late seventies, Alexander III. of Russia (then the Tsarevitch), accompanied by the Tsarevna and her sister, the Princess of Wales, visited the Exhibition in Baker Street.

On reaching the entrance to the Napoleon Rooms and the Chamber of Horrors, where an extra admission fee of sixpence is charged, my uncle, who was standing near, heard the Tsarevitch say to his companions that he had no money.

The Princess of Wales was obliged to admit that she was in the same penniless plight, while the Tsarevna exclaimed with emphasis, " *Et moi aussi ; je n'ai pas un penny dans ma poche !* "

Here, then, it may be said, was a trio of

monarchs-to-be in the amusing predicament of not having a sixpence among the three of them!

My uncle was bound to respect the royal visitors' incognito, and so could not venture to " pass them in," which, of course, he would have been very proud and happy to do.

The difficulty was overcome by one of the gentlemen in attendance on the royal party, who came up shortly afterwards and produced the necessary fees.

Princess Charles of Denmark is reported to have said many years ago, "I sometimes get tired of being a royal, especially when I am looked at and wondered at as though I were one of Madame Tussaud's wax models. I even think how glorious it must be to be able to jump on the top of a 'bus, pay my fare like any ordinary person, and have a day out. I have never tried to do so yet, but I think I shall some day."

Mention of this brings to my mind one of several visits paid to the Exhibition by the Princes of our own Royal House.

I was notified by telephone that the present Prince of Wales and his brother, Prince Albert, were visiting the Exhibition. They were received by me, and I conducted them over the place.

The royal boys needed very little " conducting," as they were soon engrossed in all they saw around them, and seldom found it necessary to address any questions to me.

I was amused to find that they preferred to dispense with the Catalogue, taking a boyish delight in recognising the figures for themselves and displaying what knowledge they possessed, which was considerable. Nor did they seem in the least concerned to know whether members of the general public recognised them, as I could see many did from the way they contrived to keep near to them.

Among the Napoleonic relics the Princes lingered an unusually long time, as if reluctant to leave them ; and the Prince of Wales betrayed so much interest in the carriage in which Napoleon was all but captured after the Battle of Waterloo that he was invited to sit in it, if he cared. Without a moment's hesitation he embraced the opportunity, and his brother joined him.

It happened that we were just then about to have the carriage glazed in, as it has been since, to protect it from ruthless souvenir hunters, whose mutilations necessitated our keeping in stock rolls of cloth of the same pattern to renew the lining from time to time.

I wonder how many people in different parts of the world now show their friends strips of cloth purporting to be taken from the original lining of the Napoleon carriage, whereas the " souvenirs " are really " relics " of the looms of Yorkshire.

The last to sit in Napoleon's carriage were the Prince of Wales and Prince Albert.

CHAPTER XXXIII

The Begum of Bhopal pays us a visit—Lord Rosebery and Lord
Annaly—Lord Randolph Churchill—Lady Beatty, Lady
Jellicoe, and Mrs. Asquith.

IT was on the 29th of June, eight years ago, that
we had a visit from the Begum of Bhopal, a lady
who rules over millions in India.

She was in London for the coronation of King
George and Queen Mary. As the Begum was a
Moslem, we were somewhat concerned as to how
we should receive Her Highness, it being rumoured
that she could not be chaperoned by one of the
opposite sex. I must deny the story that we had
to turn all the males out of the Exhibition, for
there was no occasion to do so.

The Begum was dressed in brown, with a flowing
white yashmak hanging from a quaint head-dress
shaped like a top-hat of the Leech period. This
veil, by the etiquette of her country, is worn in
the company of men, the wearer looking through
two eye-holes.

In order that the exhibits might be explained to her,
my wife and a friend of hers, Mrs. Arthur Dulcken,
who spoke Hindustani fluently, acted as guides.

Two turbaned gentlemen were in attendance, and the Begum walked between her little grandson and granddaughter, whose hands she held.

Her knowledge of English history was surprising. Even the Prince, who was only six years old, prattled about different English kings, though he insisted that the good King Alfred, shown in the neatherd's cottage, where he is being rated by the shrew for allowing her cakes to burn, was a fairy-tale like that of the Sleeping Beauty.

When the party came to the Grand Hall in which King George and Queen Mary sat arrayed in their coronation robes, with six Princesses of the Royal House standing around them, " Bara Salaam," said the Begum, as she bowed to the Emperor of India.

Before the scene which shows Queen Victoria receiving the news of her accession to the throne the little lady halted.

" She was very beautiful," she said, " and so wise and kind and sympathetic."

It was the tribute of one woman ruler to another.

" She was very beautiful," she said again, " and so small. In Bhopal we think small people beautiful."

The Begum's inches were some sixty-two.

She glanced approvingly at the model of Tom Thumb, and proudly placed her grandson by the figure of the Russian giant to accentuate her admiration for small people.

As she passed through the Chamber of Horrors, with its guillotine and gallows, she said, with some degree of satisfaction, " We do not execute in Bhopal."

" I thank you," she said, as she departed in state ; and her retainers added an official word of praise : " The Begum has found Madame Tussaud's extremely interesting."

Lord Rosebery has more than once visited Madame Tussaud's, and made a fairly long stay on each occasion.

Only very recently he and Lord Annaly, Lord-in-Waiting to the King, came to the Exhibition together. Our lecturer happened to notice them among the visitors in the building, and observed the two noblemen make a careful inspection of the exhibits, conversing in a lively manner, and occasionally calling each other's attention to models which struck them as being specially interesting.

It is, of course, difficult to judge whether they were prompted by any particular motive, or paid the visit merely to enjoy a few minutes' respite from the more serious affairs of life ; but they both minutely examined the relics of the French Revolution and, curiously enough, the figures of the criminals in the Chamber of Horrors, where they spent some considerable time.

Lord Rosebery, as a citizen of Edinburgh, called

his friend's attention to the striking figures of Burke and Hare, with the story of whose crimes Lord Rosebery must, of course, have been familiar. These ghoulish men perpetrated a series of murders in the Scottish capital in the year 1828 for the purpose of obtaining money by selling the bodies to anatomical schools as subjects for dissection.

It may not be generally known that the verb "to burke" is derived from the villainous miscreant of that name.

One would like to have heard what passed between Lord Rosebery and Lord Annaly as, having left the abode of criminals, they stopped in front of the former's portrait in the main hall of the Exhibition.

As they were leaving the building our representative, as an act of courtesy, opened the middle gate to let them pass with greater freedom, and, in doing so, said, "Good-night, my lord." Lord Rosebery smiled in response, like one who is pleased at being recognised. It was evident from their demeanour that both the peers had enjoyed their experience.

Lord Randolph Churchill once said that the two proudest moments in his life were neither his first election to Parliament nor his first appearance on the Treasury Bench, but the publication of a speech of his in leaflet form and the appearance of his effigy at Madame Tussaud's. He added that he had long wished to see how he looked there, but had never dared to go. Notwithstanding this remark he was seen in the flesh on more than one occasion at a later date sauntering through the Exhibition rooms.

That the wives of famous men invariably feel curious to see the models of their husbands goes without saying, and very many instances might be cited of their having done so. Among those who visited the Exhibition during the war were Lady Jellicoe, Lady Beatty, and Mrs. Asquith.

Lady Beatty made a very intelligent criticism of the Admiral's portrait, and as the result of her suggestions certain alterations were made.

Lady Jellicoe's criticism was quite favourable. " You have been extremely fortunate in catching my husband's expression," she said.

Mrs. Asquith did not make any comments, but her young son, who came with her, derived not a little amusement from his distinguished father's presentment, and showed his appreciation by coming again and bringing a boy friend to see it the very next day.

CHAPTER XXXIV

Tussaud's as educator—Queer questions—Wanted, a "model"
wife—Quaint extract from an Indian's diary.

AN American visitor to the Exhibition once said
to me, " You know, this show is a liberal education,
a history of Europe in kind. I never learned so
much history in any one afternoon. Why don't
you write your reminiscences ? "

I told him that I probably should do so one day,
and he replied characteristically :

" There is no time like the present. Get on
with it, and put me down as a subscriber."

A French Ambassador is reported to have said :
"A day in Tussaud's is worth a year at Oxford ;
it fixes history as no tutor could."

On more than one occasion schoolmasters have
made a similar remark with reference to the value
of the figures and exhibits in Madame Tussaud's
as a means of impressing the minds of their boys
with the episodes of history. Teachers often bring
their pupils, and I am constantly receiving
appreciative letters after a visit.

Schoolboys themselves, I have always noticed,

take the keenest possible interest in all they see, and I frequently overhear them eagerly challenging one another concerning the identity and lives of historical personages as they confront their models.

The Exhibition has been frequently consulted as an authority upon innumerable historical subjects, especially with regard to matters dealing with portraiture, biography, and costume, and many of the questions submitted might well have puzzled even the compiler of an encyclopædia. Queries are almost always coupled with an urgent request for immediate reply.

Peculiarities of well-known people are fruitful topics for inquiry. The following are a few of the questions put :

" On which side of Cromwell's face did his warts grow ? "

" Which was the arm that Nelson lost, and which was his blind eye ? "

" Was Byron's club-foot the right or the left ? "

" Did Mary, Queen of Scots, have brown eyes or blue ? "

Again : " What was the height of Napoleon ? " —the most frequent question of all.

Other popular problems relate to costume :

" Did the Black Prince really wear black armour ? Or to what was his cognomen due ? "

We were consulted during the period when preparations were in progress for the late King Edward's coronation so as to decide what was the correct tone of purple for the royal robes. As we have in our possession the robes actually worn by George IV. at that King's coronation, we allowed a broad hem on one of the trains to be unstitched, thus revealing the original colour, unchanged by exposure to dust and light.

In this connection the following quotation from Thackeray's *The Four Georges*, published in 1861, is interesting :

> Madame Tussaud has got King George's coronation robes ; is there any man now alive who would kiss the hem of that trumpery ? He sleeps since thirty years.

The same author also mentions the Exhibition in the following extract from *The Newcomes* :

> For pictures they do not seem to care much ; they thought the National Gallery a dreary exhibition, and in the Royal Academy could be got to admire nothing but the picture of M'Collop of M'Collop, by our friend of the like name : but they think Madame Tussaud's interesting exhibition of Waxwork the most delightful in London : and there I had the happiness of introducing them to our friend Mr. Frederick Bayham ; who, subsequently, on coming to this office with his valuable contributions on the Fine Arts, made particular inquiries as to their pecuniary means, and expressed himself instantly ready to bestow his hand upon the mother or daughter, provided old Mr. Binnie would make a satisfactory settlement.

On one or two other occasions our relics and historic pictures have been specially viewed by those who had charge of the arrangements, for the express purpose of settling points in regard to precedence and costume at royal functions.

Inquiries from members of the public often come about through a dispute which has ended in a wager, but many and various are the reasons that are assigned by the questioner for his query. Sometimes my correspondent is a writer of books, who wants to give a correct description of a character or incident.

This leads me to the subject of misconception, and it is surprising how deep-rooted are the inaccuracies that have crept into the minds of visitors with regard to the models they have seen in the Exhibition. Many of our patrons express themselves as absolutely certain that figures have done things which I am equally positive they never did and never could do.

What is the use of telling individuals that the originator of Hansard's Parliamentary Debates, William Cobbett, who turns his head from side to side, does not take snuff, when they insist that they have actually seen him lift his hand from his snuff-box to his nose? Yet this is a widespread fallacy.

The figure of Marat dying in his bath never has breathed; it is the bosom of the Sleeping Beauty that rises and falls as she reposes in slumber.

Neither does Henry VIII. turn his head to inspect his six wives. Those who think he does must be confusing him with the aforesaid Cobbett, although not a few readers of history think that the head of Bluff King Hal, who caused so many people to be beheaded, must itself have been " turned."

Some years ago an elderly bachelor from the Midlands called to ask whether we could make him a model of a lady based upon his own description and sketches and dressed in clothes designed by himself.

I should have attached no importance to the matter had I not, my curiosity being whetted, asked a few questions of the caller.

It then transpired that the model was to represent his ideal woman whom he had been unable to discover in real life. He was anxious to have a woman about the house " pleasing to the eye, but at the same time somewhat less loquacious than the usual run of females," as he put it.

He proposed that the model should be placed in an adjustable chair and be jointed, so that at meal-times it could sit at the head of his lonely table and at other times could recline at ease beside the fire, opposite his own armchair.

Needless to say, the commission was not accepted.

It is very natural that such an institution as Madame Tussaud's should include the "curious" among its diversified store of anecdote.

One quaint document in our archives is the published diary of an Indian officer, Jemadar, No. 1427, Abdur Razzak, of the 15th Madras Lancers, from

P

which I give the following extract relating to a visit
he paid to the Exhibition :

On the 5th June, 1893, we went to see the Wax Work
"Madame Tussaud," where we first saw a woman in red
dress with a basket full of different kinds of flowers all
made in wax with her, which was very difficult to make out
that she was an image, but when we entered the building
we saw lots of images of emperors and kings, and remarkable
persons both men and women with rich and poor dresses on.

I really say that I was very much admired to see these
images, and was in many places in the buildings mistook
the visitors to be of them when they were standing still,
but when they moved was very much ashamed on account
of my misunderstanding ; by this we made our minds to
be little far from both the images and the visitors and
servants in the building.

We saw the throne of Her Majesty just the same we have
seen on the 9th May, 1893, besides this one more image
in shape with Her Majesty in a room writing something
on a table with a candle on it, and this too quite astonishing.

We also saw a gentleman on elephant's back in a jungle
has hunted a tiger, the pair of which attacked the elephant
round its trunk taking to him and the elephant putting
its head down and a gentleman on it, aiming to fire on the
tiger.

We saw a room in which were the images of almost all
the assassinators with the particulars of their deeds. We
also saw a place in which all the weapons, etc., to take
revenge of assassinators, such as scabbard, hanging, &c.

CHAPTER XXXV

PEOPLE sometimes ask me how my portraits are
taken, and how my subjects sit to me.

It is very much with my work as it is with
the work of a sculptor. There is practically only
this distinction in principle—the sculptor reproduces
his work in marble or bronze, and I execute mine
in wax, both working from a first impression in
clay. Added to this there is, of course, a difference
in the matter of treatment.

Sitters have their own peculiar characteristics,
and often require humouring.

I once wrote to Miss Ellen Terry, asking her to
do me the honour of sitting to me ; and she replied
that she would be pleased to do so, making no
appointment.

A few days afterwards the vivacious actress
found her way to my studio door without anyone
to guide her, and how she got there has always
puzzled me. I was engrossed in some urgent
work, when a rap came and Miss Terry sailed in,
all smiles and animation.

She did not introduce herself. There was no need. I knew her instantly, as I supposed she imagined I should. It was a very hot day, and she said, " I am positively dying for a cup of tea."

She told me she was just clearing off all her visiting arrears before sailing, and added : " You see, Mr. Tussaud, I have not forgotten you."

The cup that cheers was very soon brewed, and Miss Terry saw that I noticed a gauntlet on her right hand as she raised the cup to her lips.

" I met with a slight accident on the stage," she said.

I wish I could recall some of her delightful chat, and I regret that I did not keep a diary instead of trusting entirely to memory. However, I may derive some consolation from the conclusion, arrived at by an old and experienced literary friend, that it is seldom what has been forgotten would have been worth writing about had it been remembered.

When I had finished modelling, and not till then, Miss Terry apologised for being in a hurry, and as she took her departure I found myself wondering by what secret art or gift she could conjure up so much mirth and sprightliness when the thermometer was registering ninety in the shade.

After Miss Terry had gone my eye happened to catch the chair on which she had been sitting, and I discovered that the back legs were within an eighth of an inch of the edge of the high dais.

I trembled to think of what might have happened to the actress if the chair had fallen to the floor while she occupied it. I suppose the reason for its position having changed from that in which it was originally placed was that the actress, who could hardly be described as a reposeful " sitter," had shifted it in her restlessness.

The carpenter had omitted to fix the fillet which should have been placed to preclude any risk of the chair falling from its elevated position.

Only a few months ago Lady Bancroft, speaking at a matinée in aid of King George's Pension Fund for Actors, made an amusing allusion to Madame Tussaud's.

She had just been listening to the dialogue between Peg Woffington, played by Irene Vanburgh, and Triplet, and she said :

" When it was arranged that my husband should come from his retirement to play the part of Triplet, we were very much exercised where to find his old costume.

" Then, all at once, we remembered the last time we saw that costume was at Madame Tussaud's.

" I said, ' Of course you have been melted down by this time.'

" He said, ' What do you think they have made of me ? Perhaps Marshal Foch, perhaps President Poincaré, perhaps President Wilson. I only hope my figure has not been melted down to something in the Chamber of Horrors.' "

None laughed more heartily than the King at Lady Bancroft's story.

It was in the spring of 1889 that the Bancrofts gave me several sittings. The merry laughter of the actress made the time pass quickly and my work a real joy.

When the models of Mr. and Mrs. Bancroft were added to the Exhibition, in the characters of Peg Woffington and Triplet in *Masks and Faces*, reference to this was made in our Easter announcement.

Sir Squire Bancroft tells the following story in this connection :

" A young man from the country visited the Exhibition on Easter Monday of that year, and went straight to the Chamber of Horrors. He said he wanted to see the ' *squire who murdered a triplet* ' ! "

They tell me that Henry Irving came to see his portrait a year after I had modelled him, but, unfortunately, I missed the great actor that day.

Mention of Irving takes my mind back rather a long way, to the time when I had the pleasure of introducing his model and that of Miss Ellen Terry to the Exhibition. They were on the eve of making their first journey across the Atlantic, and they cheerfully consented to enable me to let the public see them in their absence.

Irving was an ideal sitter, as might be expected of a great actor. He adapted himself to my requirements in every detail, and gave me to feel that he took great pleasure in my work. I very soon became aware of Irving's kindliness of heart and his sympathy with an artist at his labours.

Conversation turned upon the question of insuring Madame Tussaud's against fire, and Irving remarked that money would be a very poor compensation for the loss of our irreplaceable collection, especially having regard to the relics of Napoleon and the heads of the French revolutionaries.

The actor told me of an alarming experience he had while acting at the Lyceum Theatre.

The play was nearing its most dramatic climax when he noticed that fire had broken out in the "sky borders," and the fear of a panic in the audience rose in his mind lest any member of it should chance to see the flames.

He admitted that it was an ordeal that required all his courage to face without betraying signs of anxiety, but he succeeded in continuing to play his part without a single person in the front of the house suspecting that there was any cause for alarm.

Fortunately, the stage carpenters and attendants were able to extinguish the fast-spreading flames without any interruption. The curtain was eventually rung down on an applauding audience, quite oblivious of the danger that had threatened.

Irving lighted his pipe on his departure, which set me thinking that he would have enjoyed a smoke during the sitting, but was too courteous and considerate to suggest one. He told me he hoped, on his return from America, to visit the Exhibition and see his portrait. He came and saw it, but I did not see him.

Sir Henry used to employ the same cabman to take him to the theatre each evening. He asked him once if he had ever seen him act, and, the man replying in the negative, Irving gave him five shillings with which the cabman could procure seats for himself and his wife in the pit.

On the following day the actor asked the driver what he thought of him on the stage.

" To tell you the truth," said the ingenuous jehu, " we didn't go."

" Not go," said Irving, " when I gave you the money for the seats ! "

" Well, sir," said the man, " it was this way. It was my missus's birthday, and I asked her which she would prefer to do—go to see you act, or go to Madame Tussaud's, and she said she preferred the waxworks."

Irving often related this story against himself with the greatest gusto, enjoying it quite as much as his hearers did.

On many occasions Madame Tussaud's has been of service to the stage.

When the late W. G. Wills, the author of *Jane Shore*, a prolific playwright in his day, was at the height of his popularity, my father was approached by Mr. Coleman, manager of the

Queen's Theatre, Long Acre, to produce for him a figure of Charles I.

The reason of this request was, surely, one of the strangest that ever entered the brain of even the most enterprising of theatrical managers.

Mr. George Rignold was playing at that theatre a drama, written by Wills, entitled *Cromwell*. This play was the successor of another by the same dramatist, namely, *Charles I.*, in which Irving played the part of the King, and confirmed the reputation he had made in *The Bells*.

A bargain had been struck that if *Charles I.* succeeded, Wills should write *Cromwell* for Mr. Coleman. *Charles I.* proved a great success at the Lyceum, but *Cromwell* was a comparative failure at the Queen's.

I come now to the reason of Mr. Coleman's request for a waxen model of the King.

He said he wanted it to repose in the coffin on the stage to stimulate the imagination of the actor, Mr. Rignold, when rendering the long oration delivered by Cromwell in the presence of the dead monarch.

The model was furnished with every detail, even to the clothing in which the body was attired. I was afterwards told that only the manager, the actor, and my father were aware of the realistic plan that had been devised to accentuate an actor's eloquence.

CHAPTER XXXVI

MR. G. R. SIMS was a cheery, entertaining sitter;
not, perhaps, what most artists would consider a
helpful one. His active mind busied itself with
every object of interest around him. He would
know all about them, and tell each off with some
droll quip or whimsical jest.

I have spent many a bright hour with " Dagonet "
—yes, even including those spent with him in the
Chamber of Horrors.

I once chanced to have a book of his (the *Dagonet
Ballads*) in my hand when he came into my studio,
and I asked him to sign his name in it. Without
a moment's hesitation he wrote:

> DEAR TUSSAUD,
>   I'm a model man.
>   You're a modeller.
>   Yours truly,
>   G. R. SIMS.

Soon after we had decided to add Mr. Sims's
figure to the Exhibition, Mrs. G. A. Sala
happened to meet him, and questioned him as to

the sensations he experienced in picturing himself as a waxen celebrity.

" I feel very frightened indeed," he promptly replied, " and more than that, exceedingly sorry that I ever promised to become a waxwork, for I have been told since that if the public grow weary of your presence, or the Tussauds get offended with you, they melt you down, and build up a more popular fellow out of your dripping. Nasty idea, very ! "

Mrs. Sala said it certainly *was* a very nasty idea ; but if there were any truth in the melting-down story, G. R. could enjoy the satisfaction of thinking that he might have arisen in his waxen grandeur from the " dripping " of someone less popular than himself.

Mr. Sims said that so long as the public only stuck pins into him, or stamped on his toes, he did not mind ; but he should feel it very much if they were to bang him about the head with an umbrella, or take him by the collar and shake him.

It must have been in the early winter of the year 1891, while I was modelling him, that Mr. Sims had the following interesting and somewhat unpleasant experience, which he himself describes. He says :

" I have been penetrating the secrets of Tussaud's lately, and had a specially quiet half-hour alone with the murderers in the Chamber of Horrors, just to see what it was like.

" The idea came to me one night when I had been sitting late to Mr. John Tussaud. I wanted to see what it would feel like to be all alone with those awful people with only one dim jet of gas lighting up their fearful features.

" After the door was shut I walked about and whistled, and stared defiantly at William Corder and James Bloomfield Rush, and even went so far as to address M. Eyraud in French. But wandering about in the semi-darkness I stumbled and fell, and when I got up and looked around me I found I was in Mrs. Pearcey's kitchen.

" Then I made one wild rush at the closed door, and hammered at it until the kindly watchman came and let me out. I never want to be shut up alone at night in the Chamber of Horrors again as long as I live."

Humorously describing my studios at the time, Mr. Sims says :

" At Madame Tussaud's I am at present in rather a curious condition. There is a good deal of the Thames mystery about me. It is not given to every man to see his legs in one room, his hands hanging up in another, and his head on a shelf, looking about anxiously for his body.

" I can't say I quite like looking at my head on a shelf. It suggests decapitation and Madame de Lamballe's head on a pike as Louis caught sight of it when the mob held it up at the window.

" But I am assured that I shall be put together

next week, and that my limbs will once more be found together as Nature intended they should be.

" I don't know what that Scotch sixpenny which refers to me in highly uncomplimentary terms about seven times in every column will say, but the exigencies of space at the Marylebone Museum have compelled the management to put me next to Lord Tennyson. I am sure that this will be such a shock to my modesty that I shall go hot and melt the very first day that the weather is at all warm.

" Fortunately, I shall have a brother journalist to support me and keep me in countenance, for while Lord Tennyson is seated writing poetry in his study, Mr. George Augustus Sala in *his* study sits next door to him, dashing off one of his brilliant leaders for the *Daily Telegraph*. It is in a study built up on the other side of Lord Tennyson that the visitor to Madame Tussaud's will at an early date find himself face to face with ' Dagonet.' "

There George R. Sims has been seated ever since. Twenty-eight years ago ! Time has wrought many changes, but during the whole of that period I have uninterruptedly enjoyed Mr. Sims's valued friendship.

George Augustus Sala sat to me about the same time, and a very good sitter he was. The celebrated journalist lived in a flat at Victoria Street, Westminster, where I called on him, and I remember his saying to me with pride :

" I'm taking up modern Greek in my sixtieth year. What do you think I am reading? I am reading an excellent account in Greek of the Stanfield Hall murder."

During the autumn of 1889 I had seen a good deal of Mr. Sala, for we were at that time discussing the details for the rewriting of our Exhibition Catalogue.

He had always taken a great interest in Madame Tussaud's, and, like many other literary men, had found it useful as a place of reference on matters of portraiture and costume. He entered upon the scheme for producing a better and larger Catalogue with great enthusiasm, but I soon discovered that the work was hardly likely to receive that equable treatment necessary for a book of the kind.

There were certain subjects his mind positively ran riot on, while others scarcely aroused the slightest interest.

Marie Antoinette and Mary, Queen of Scots, stirred his imagination most of all, and to the ill-fated Queen of Louis XVI. he reverted so often that it seemed the book was likely to be over-weighted with matter dealing with her sad career, to the exclusion of so much else of vital importance to our handbook.

Whenever he stood in front of the decapitated head of Marie Antoinette he always contemplated it in silence—and invariably passed from it without making any remark, as if it were a subject too sad for ordinary comment.

" I have done the Marie Antoinette biography," greeted me long before the work had been definitely agreed upon, and six or seven pages of essay were pressed into my hands as an accomplished undertaking that positively left no room for further consideration. This matter was printed in full in our Catalogue, and remained there until the difficulty in procuring paper during the war necessitated its temporary elimination. It is, perhaps, the best thing, from a purely literary point of view, that Sala ever wrote.

It was inevitable that so prominent a figure in the religious world as the late General Booth should find a place in Madame Tussaud's Exhibition.

I went to see the General at the instance of some of his friends, who thought that the portrait of him already included would be all the better for being brought up to date. I recollect being impressed by General Booth's force of character as manifested alike in his manner and in his appearance. He had a keen eye and classic aquiline features.

Though he made no mention of the matter himself, it was pretty plainly hinted to me that permission to include the General's portrait should be accompanied by some expression of gratitude on the part of the Exhibition authorities " for the good of the cause."

I also went to Exeter Hall to study the General's demeanour while addressing a large audience.

What I remember mostly about that visit was that a "converted" sailor mounted the platform and made a rambling speech. So frank were the confessions of the artless tar that General Booth found it necessary to bundle him unceremoniously off the platform, to the great amusement of the congregation.

CHAPTER XXXVII

THE most restless of all my sitters was the Right Honourable John Burns, when he was plain John Burns.

I modelled him in the year 1889 or 1890, at the time of the great Dock Strike. Mr. Burns was then throwing all his magnetic personality into the cause of the workers, and he brought some of that magnetic personality into my studio. Only in a technical sense did he " sit " to me. He was walking and talking all the time.

These were very turbulent days, and Mr. Burns had figured in the Trafalgar Square riots. Shipowners and shipbuilders—and everybody, I imagine, having more than £500 a year—were the objects of his implacable distrust. He was a younger and poorer man then.

Mr. Burns wore the blue reefer suit which had survived the jostlings of many a crowd, but he did not bring to my studio the famous straw hat of which so much was written in the Press at that time. When I spoke to him about the hat he rather fenced the question, and to this day I believe that hat to be somewhere in Mr. Burns's possession as a treasured souvenir of his stressful past. I have never seen Mr. Burns wearing any other kind of clothes than blue serge.

I struck a bargain with the dockers' champion that he should let me have the suit he was wearing with which to clothe his portrait in the Exhibition, and so complete the realism of the model. Mr. Burns demurred at first, and then it appeared he had an extremely good reason for doing so. It was the only suit he possessed, and we agreed that I should have it as soon as I provided him with a new one to take its place on his own back.

Mr. Burns told the story of this transaction in reply to an interrupter at a public meeting.

" Where did you get that suit ? " asked the interrogator.

" I got it," said Mr. Burns frankly, " from Madame Tussaud's. When my portrait was put in the Exhibition you may, or you may not, have noticed that it was wearing my old suit. As I had no other clothes the management gave me the suit I am wearing now, and I hope you will agree that I made a pretty good bargain."

The audience cheered the speaker and booed the heckler.

Mr. Burns's portrait has been brought up to date since then, but it still wears the old reefer suit, and the fact of this being out of the fashion and rather skimpy only adds to the effectiveness of the picture by recalling the working man the late Sir Henry Campbell-Bannerman raised to Cabinet rank.

They tell me Mr. Burns is getting white, but when I modelled him his hair was black and plentiful.

Judy commemorated the suit incident in the following verse, depicting Burns making figure eights on the ice :

> 'Ave ye seen Johnny Burns
> Strikin' figgers on the hice ?
> 'Ave ye seen his twists and turns ?—
> Sure, an' can't he do it nice !
> In his Tussaud's suit of navy blue
> 'N' his famous old straw hat,
> With his Hacmes 'n' his knobstick too,
> A reg'lar 'ristocrat !

A contrast to Mr. Burns, though possibly of similar socialistic opinions, was Mr. George Bernard Shaw, whom I long wanted to sit to me.

I had not made the acquaintance of the brilliant satirist, and somehow hesitated about approaching him. Eventually I wrote to Mr. Shaw making known my wish, and, without delay, I received from him a good-humoured letter, in which he said that it would give him much pleasure to " join the company of the Immortals."

A little later he wrote making an appointment, and, in due course, Mr. Shaw came to my studio and gave me a delightful hour of his company.

He took up his position on the dais in the most natural manner, and there was nothing more for me to do than proceed with my modelling. I do not know who was the more amused, Mr. Shaw or myself—I by his sayings, and he by the novelty of the situation.

He talked freely as I went on with my work, and one thing among his many whimsical sayings I well remember :

" I took to writing with the object of obtaining a living without having to work for it, but I have long since realised that I made a great mistake."

As we walked through the Exhibition he took a general interest in all he saw, but it was the Napoleonic relics that detained him, as is generally the case with distinguished people.

I thought I detected a certain shyness about Mr. Shaw in the Chamber of Horrors. He was very reserved, and surveyed the faces of degenerate men and women without offering any criticism. I remember that the crafty, and yet not wholly repulsive, face of Charles Peace engaged Mr. Shaw's attention several minutes.

I have no knowledge whether Mr. Shaw ever called to see his portrait. It is quite likely that he did, and it is no less likely that his visit passed unobserved.

I was much interested in modelling a quartette of leading suffragettes, Mrs. Pankhurst, Mrs. Pethick Lawrence, Miss Christabel Pankhurst, and Miss Annie Kenney.

The group is conspicuously shown in the Grand Hall to-day. The ladies came separately, several mornings, and took as much interest as I did in the production of their portraits, a process that was in no sense tedious, as their conversation whiled away the time most pleasantly.

I very soon became aware that the suffragette on the political warpath is a very different woman from the suffragette in other circumstances.

None of them in the least degree frightened me or hectored me ; in fact, political questions were discussed by them in the quietest, most sensible, and most intelligent manner, giving me the impression then that the extension of the vote to women would not find such women unqualified to make reasonable use of the privilege so long withheld from them.

After the figures were added to the Exhibition, two of the four ladies very good-humouredly hinted to me that the portraits were not very flattering. I remember the ladies in question coming to see the group, and I promised I would make what alterations seemed possible and desirable. As I have not heard from them since, I gather that the likenesses have proved satisfactory.

Months later, after a batch of laughing damsels

had left the building, a paper disc, bearing the words "Votes for Women," was discovered fixed to a button on Mr. Asquith's coat.

It was soon after the figures of the quartette had been placed in the Exhibition that an incident occurred which comes to me through the medium of a Fleet Street artist in black and white attached to a well-known paper.

This gentleman had been instructed to attend a meeting some distance away from town for the purpose of taking some sketches of Miss Christabel Pankhurst, who was announced to speak. Having left things till the last moment, he discovered, to his dismay, that he had missed his train, and, not knowing what to do, he was bewailing his misfortune to a fellow artist, when the latter slapped him on the back and said :

" Never mind, old fellow, you just go to Tussaud's Exhibition and take as many pictures of the fair Christabel's figure as you like. The model is a speaking likeness, and you can take it from me that the sketches will be all right ; they will be quite as good as if drawn from life."

The advice was no sooner given than acted upon, and the result, I am told, was most satisfactory.

Another sitter was Mr. T. W. Burgess, who came to my studio a few days after he swam the Channel.

The burly Yorkshireman laughed as he entered and remarked :

" I am in pretty good training, but I would rather swim the Channel again than sit still for you, Mr. Tussaud. However, I will do the best I can."

He sold the clothes he took off before he entered the water, and these clothes are worn by his portrait, now in the Exhibition. He also parted with the goggles and indiarubber cap he had worn during his swim, and the cup from which he took nourishment. Unfortunately one of Burgess's too ardent " admirers " purloined his hero's cup from us.

CHAPTER XXXVIII

Bank Holiday queues—Cup-tie day—Gentlemen from the north
—Bachelor beanfeasts—The Member for Oldham—A scare.

THE four regular Bank Holidays of the year are great occasions at Madame Tussaud's.

On each of them the precincts of Tussaud's show signs of activity long before the average Londoner is astir. The length of any of the queues has never been actually measured, but it is no exaggeration to say that the people have frequently waited four and five deep in a line extending almost a quarter of a mile—from the doors of the Exhibition to the gates of Regent's Park.

The crowd at these times consists mainly of Londoners from all the outlying districts of the Metropolis, for Madame Tussaud's has always been in great favour as a holiday resort for the multitude. Parents also bring their children in great numbers, and the holiday crowds continue to come for days after.

There is, however, at least one morning in the year when the portals of the Exhibition are literally teeming with life while the citizens are slumbering in bed.

On Easter Monday, Whit-Monday, the August Bank Holiday, and even on Boxing Day, holiday-makers may be seen at an early hour waiting in a queue, yet no comparison may be made between these crowds and those of the Cup-tie mornings I have witnessed at the Exhibition.

This day brings into London tens of thousands of men and boys from the densely populated manufacturing towns and mining areas of Lancashire, Yorkshire, Durham, and Northumberland. These football enthusiasts arrive in the Metropolis as early in the morning as two, three, and four o'clock on the day of the Crystal Palace carnival.

It has always seemed to me that Madame Tussaud's has received the lion's share of patronage during the long interval between the arrival of the cheap excursion trains at the great railway stations and the time when the Cup-tie is played in the after-noon. The attendance at these hours is extra-ordinary, and the appearance of a house of entertainment in full swing so early in the morning has an indescribably weird and garish effect.

These north country patrons of ours take up position on the steps of the entrance, and pass the time taking refreshments brought with them from their homes. Though weary with their journey, they are always cheery and well-behaved, and the way in which they banter each other in the broad accents of Oldham, Manchester, Leeds, Bradford, Sheffield, Halifax, Newcastle, etc., has many a time afforded me a good deal of interest and diversion.

I have often stood on the broad open staircase and looked down upon the swarming hundreds in the entrance-hall and the refreshment rooms, and it is a happy experience to dwell on that there has never been occasion to rebuke any of them for roughness or want of good behaviour. It is peculiarly true of the country cousin, so far as my experience of him goes, that he never indulges in horse-play when he comes to Madame Tussaud's.

There is, however, one very striking contrast between the crowd on a Bank Holiday and that on a Cup-tie day, and this is due to the circumstances that the followers of football do not bring their womenfolk or children with them on the occasion of these " bachelor " beanfeasts—a concession, I presume, made to their men by the wives and sweethearts of the north.

Not by a long way do all these excursionists go to see the great football finals at the Palace. Quite a large proportion, taking advantage of the cheap fares, come to see London and its many sights which the average Londoner proverbially overlooks.

It has more than once been remarked by the Exhibition attendants that many Cup-tie visitors spend the greater part of the day at Madame Tussaud's, lingering for hours among the relics of Napoleon and the figures and exhibits of the Chamber of Horrors, without having the slightest intention of venturing so far as to see the football contest played.

It is a mistake to imagine that the working classes of the north are ignorant of English history, or not concerned with it ; and if that impression exists, I should like to correct it. I doubt whether any class takes a keener interest in the Hall of Kings, or makes more use of the information provided by the Catalogue.

The " trippers," " country cousins," or whatever one likes to call them, seldom pester the Exhibition attendants with queries, for what one does not know another does. The Catalogues are taken away for further perusal, and one may often search the whole Exhibition in vain the next morning for one that has been discarded.

All day long groups of Cup-tie trippers stand about the Sleeping Beauty, not only for her sake, but also for the sake of Madame Tussaud, whose figure stands at Madame St. Amaranthe's head, while at her feet sits William Cobbett, wearing his old beaver hat, and holding in his hand the snuff-box which legend credits him with passing to visitors on some weird occasions.

Men from Oldham naturally show special interest in Cobbett, who was, in his day, Member of Parliament for that town.

Cobbett sits on a red upholstered ottoman, with room enough for two other persons, and on a certain Cup-tie day two travel-stained, tired men sat down by him, and, noticing that he moved his head from side to side, took him to be alive. They addressed questions to him, and jumped up very hurriedly as he jerked his head and looked blankly at them through his horn spectacles.

The only two figures in the Exhibition that make any pretence of life are William Cobbett and the Sleeping Beauty.

A wonderful self-made man was Cobbett, who began life as a living scarecrow, armed with a shot-gun, in the employment of a farmer, and, after being, among other things, sergeant-major, won a great reputation as a writer of English prose, and attained the distinction of adding M.P. to his name in those days when Parliamentary honours were less easily achieved than they are to-day.

To be sure, the figures of statesmen have always interested Cup-tie crowds, for the provincial is much more of a politician than the Londoner.

So also literary men like Scott, Dickens, Tennyson, Burns, and Kipling come in for much attention; more, perhaps, than portraits of the clergy.

Sportsmen, too, such as W. G. Grace, Fred Archer, and " Tommy Lipton "—the last-mentioned for his America Cup performances—receive enough notice on Cup-tie days to maintain a good average of appreciation for the year.

As on Bank Holidays, so on Cup-tie days, there are always many more live than wax figures in the Chamber of Horrors from morning till night.

Indeed, I have seen the place so crowded that it was difficult to distinguish the effigies from the awestricken observers.

Sometimes I have taken a walk round the Exhibition after it was closed on the night of the Cup-tie to see that all was right.   Once I was called in haste to the Chamber of Horrors, where a stranger had been found asleep in a dark corner.   After he had been roused and escorted outside, the scared fellow made off as if he had had the hangman at his heels.   A return ticket from Bolton was picked up where he had lain.   But the man from Bolton had bolted, and did not return to claim the ticket.

CHAPTER XXXIX

ONCE in its long history Madame Tussaud's
Exhibition opened on a Sunday—not, however,
to the general public.

The occasion was special and, in a way, mysterious.
It had to do with one of the most dramatic person-
alities of the Chinese Empire and Republic.

A message reached me late on a Saturday night
that Dr. Sun Yat Sen, the first President of the
Chinese Republic, wished to visit the Exhibition
on the following Sunday morning. I was unable to
receive him in person, but arranged that an attendant should represent me.

The attendant knew nothing of the name of the
visitor till he saw him looking at his own portrait
and calling the attention of General Homer Lee—
an American soldier holding high rank in the
Chinese Army—who accompanied him, to the
dimple in the chin of the model by placing his
finger smilingly on the dimple in his own chin.

This was in the year 1911, and Sun Yat Sen was passing through London on his way from America to take up his presidential duties.

His visit to the Exhibition had been planned by Dr. (now Sir James) Cantlie, of Harley Street, to whom Sun Yat Sen owed—the greatest of all debts of gratitude—his life.

For it was this same Sun Yat Sen who, eleven years before, was liberated through the exertions of Dr. Cantlie from his prison in the Chinese Legation at Portland Place, a few minutes' walk from Madame Tussaud's.

What would have happened to him but for the fact that Dr. Cantlie's intervention resulted in Sun Yat Sen's release through Lord Salisbury's representations to the Chinese authorities can only be conjectured.

It was discovered at the time that a ship had been chartered in the Thames for the removal of Sun Yat Sen to China on a charge of treason against the Emperor—the same Emperor whose successor, under a republican form of government, Sun Yat Sen was destined to be.

Particulars were also disclosed regarding the manner of his incarceration at the Chinese Legation. He was inveigled into the place by the lures of hospitality, and, once inside, the officials relegated him to an apartment which they kept locked for many days.

It was only through Sun Yat Sen's friendship

with Dr. Cantlie, whose suspicions were aroused by
" inside " information, that the British authorities
learned of Sun Yat Sen's fate and took steps to
have him set free.

When the hero of this adventure visited Madame
Tussaud's on the Sunday morning in question to
see his model, I wondered what his reason could be,
and asked myself whether it had anything to do
with the adapting of his disguise, while travelling
from this country to China, at a time when his life
must have been in danger.

Perhaps, after all, it was nothing more than the
natural curiosity which attracts people whose
portraits have been recently added to come and
see them. The Eastern mind may not differ from
the Western in this very human respect.

Touching and dramatic in the extreme was the
incident which accompanied the unveiling of the
tableau representing the Gordon Highlanders
storming the Heights of Dargai. Lieutenant-Colonel
Mathias's words were on all lips at the time :

" That position must be taken at any cost ; the
Gordon Highlanders will take it."

Mrs. Mathias was present with her son and
daughter at the supper we gave to celebrate the
event, and a piper played " The Cock of the North "
to recall the deed of the wounded piper who fired
his comrades on to victory and was awarded the
V.C. When his father's words were recited, young

THE CHILDREN'S LORD MAYOR.
Sir William Treloar entertains his little friends at Madame
Tussaud's, 24th January, 1907.

[To face p. 24

Mathias sprang to his feet and thrilled all present by saluting in true military fashion.

One of the brightest of red-letter days in Madame Tussaud's romantic story was the 24th of January, 1907, when Sir William Treloar, " the children's Mayor," accompanied by several local Mayors, drove to the Exhibition in all the panoply of civic state to give éclat to the visit of fifteen hundred boys and girls of the poorest of the poor, whom we made our guests.

How richly the Right Honourable the Lord Mayor of London enjoyed himself on that occasion, like the large-hearted man he is, and how pre-eminently happy he was among the waifs and strays, many of whom were cripples, whose lives he has done so much to brighten ! Sir John Kirk, of the Ragged School Union, was also there, beaming with joy among his little beneficiaries. I remember Sir William Treloar pointing to his civic headgear and calling out to the children, " How do you like my Dick Turpin hat ? "

Tea-tables were laid all among the figures, and the picture produced in this way was both striking and amusing as the young people laughed and chatted by the side of the approving mutes. Perhaps the remark which seemed to create the greatest fun was when the Lord Mayor said he would like to see his Sheriffs in the Chamber of Horrors.

It was very touching to observe the boys loyally and reverently take off their caps in front of the little

R

alcove in which Queen Victoria sits, as someone has said, " signing dispatches all day long." At the close of the happy day the halls and corridors of the Exhibition rang with the shrill treble of fifteen hundred young voices singing " For he's a jolly good fellow," followed by " Hip, hip, hooray; the donkey's run away."

A tragedy happened that day not far away, in Westbourne Grove, which caused the gentlemen of the Press who attended the function to leave the Exhibition rather hurriedly. News came of the murder of Mr. William Whiteley, the Universal Provider.

CHAPTER XL

MANY of our visitors will remember the model of the policeman which stands at the entrance to the main gallery in the Exhibition. Hundreds—I might say thousands—of visitors have been "taken in" by this lifelike officer, who is the embodiment of a genial bobby prepared at any moment to show the way or tell the time.

The fame of this nameless policeman has extended to practically all the grown-ups who bring their children to see the figures, and many times in the day we see laughing parents watching the nonplussed expression on the faces of their offspring whom they have prevailed upon to go and ask where a certain model is to be found.

Immediately opposite is the figure of the pro-gramme-seller in somnolent mood, who is frequently offered sixpence for a Catalogue she cannot sell. It is the would-be customer that is sold.

It is most amusing to observe how many adults are deceived who seem to pride themselves on their discernment. For example, on Bank Holidays it is customary to have a number of real live constables on duty to regulate the crowd and give directions.

Bobby has a keen sense of humour, and some of them, entering into the spirit of the situation, now and again stand stock-still in the most natural attitude they can command. Not once, but frequently, a visitor, in passing with his friends, has, with an air of superior knowledge, pushed the ferrule of his stick or umbrella into the supposed figure's side, to be startled by the model's ejaculating, " Now then, young man, enough of that."

There is a mystery which has never been cleared up, and that is whether it was a policeman or a burglar who left a bull's-eye lantern in the Exhibition studio ; but it is quite clear that the intruder, whoever he was, fled from the place in fright.

A portrait of the Marquis of Hartington had just been finished, and left fully clothed and ready to be transferred to the Exhibition. By an oversight the door of the studio was left unfastened, and on our return in the morning it was found to have been opened.

On the floor, at the feet of the model of the Marquis, lay a bull's-eye lantern that evidently had been dropped by its owner as he rushed from the place. The probability is that the policeman, or the burglar, had flashed his lamp on the figure and had been scared to find, as he thought, a man—

or a spectre—confronting him. No claim was ever made for the lamp.

It is not an unusual thing that visitors who wish to save expense should bring with them an old Catalogue which they have treasured up at home for a future visit. This is not a safe plan, for with the addition of new figures the older ones have to be re-numbered. As a result the visitors in question are sometimes misled, as was the lady in the following story told by a Londoner.

He related that he had occasion to take a country cousin to the Exhibition, and she took with her an old Catalogue.

He paid little attention to her describing King Edward IV. as King Henry VIII., and exclaiming that she did not know Queen Mary of Scots dressed like a man. But when she said, " Well, I never ! I always thought Gladstone was a man, though my brothers call him an old woman," then he felt in-terested, and proceeded to investigate. There it was, sure enough ; the model No. 63 was the figure of an old lady, but in the out-of-date Catalogue No. 63 was " William Ewart Gladstone."

Sometimes we get a rough old country farmer who has got it into his head that everyone in our Exhibition has committed some crime or other.

Visitors, when audibly perusing their Catalogue, are sometimes a source of entertainment to others who overhear them, owing to the curious mistakes they make. One day a jolly-looking countryman came to a standstill before the figure of Henry IV. of France, described in our Catalogue as "Henri Quatre." "'Enry Carter," said he; "'oo did 'e kill?" and, finding the gentleman in question innocent of murder, he turned away with a disappointed expression, but evidently with a fixed determination to discover a genuine criminal somewhere else.

Not only children, but also their elders, constantly mistake the policeman, the programme-seller, and the sleeping attendant for living people; but few children are so simple as the little maiden who, glancing awestruck down the long array of very lifelike effigies of good, bad, and indifferent individuals, asked her mother in a whisper how they were killed before being stuffed.

One day a lady was explaining the different groups to her young nephew. Pointing to one, she said, " Freddy, this is the Transvaal crisis. Here are President Kruger, Mr. Cecil Rhodes, and Dr. Jameson; all those people are alive."

Indicating the next group, she said, " This is the execution of Mary, Queen of Scots; all these people are dead."

" I do not see any difference between the live ones and the dead ones," replied the young hopeful to his auntie, assuming a puzzled expression.

There is no accounting for the actions of children. Several youngsters, for instance, have been observed slyly pinching the figures to see if any were alive.

The story is also told of a small girl who, when asked what she had done with her sweets, replied that she had given them to the baby in the cradle— Prince Edward of Wales.

A child was lost, and found concealed behind the figure of the Sleeping Beauty, trying to discover the mechanism that makes Madame St. Amaranthe's bosom rise and fall.

Of children's stories there is no end at Madame Tussaud's.

Sir Ernest Shackleton once told some amusing stories at a dinner of the Alpine Ski Club.

He said his own small boy was terribly bored with expedition talk. He told his mother that he wanted to hear of something really exciting. " I don't want to know anything more about papa," he declared ; " tell me about the baby who was drowned in his bath." Was the boy thinking of Marat, the evil genius of the French Revolution, whom Charlotte Corday stabbed at his ablutions ?

Sir Ernest said that his wife and son had recently been to see his model at Madame Tussaud's, but the child took more interest in General Tom Thumb sitting on the palm of the Russian giant's hand than he did in the portrait of his father.

" Two ladies," the explorer said, "were standing by my figure, and the younger one observed, ' That's Latham, the airman.'

" ' No,' replied the other, ' that is not Latham ; it is the man, you know, who went to the North Pole.

"It is experiences such as these that keep a man modest," said Sir Ernest. The ladies had forgotten his name and the object of his expedition, which was in the Antarctic and not the Arctic region —a distinction of minor importance to the general public perhaps.

In the days of the Boer War the children of an illustrious couple who were touring the world fell, childlike, to discussing the presents their parents would bring home for them.

"I know what I want," said the youngest of them. "I want old Kruger's hat and whiskers, and I believe papa will bring them to me, because I want to send them to Madame Tussaud's."

Mr. Cyril Maude, the actor, was taken to the Exhibition when a small boy, and it is recorded of him that the visit inspired him with the determination to become an actor. If that were so, then we may congratulate ourselves.

Some years ago a lady wrote to say that when scolding her child for being naughty, and impressing upon her that bad little girls would not go to heaven, the child naïvely replied, "Well, mother, I can't expect to go everywhere, but I've been to Madame Tussaud's."

CHAPTER XLI

Crime may be secret, but never secure.—OLD PROVERB.

IN citing the old aphorism that society itself creates the crimes that most beset it, we shall in no way be tempted to regard the popularity of the Chamber of Horrors as due to any desire on the part of the people to visit the place with the object of gazing upon the result of their own handiwork.

An inquiry into the motives that induce the public to visit this gloomy chamber scarcely comes within the scope of this work. But that a very large number *do* visit the place in the course of each year, and that they cannot be deemed to belong to any particular class, but represent, without distinction, *all* classes of society, we may, of our own certain knowledge, aver without the slightest hesitation.

Were we, however, if only from an abstract point of view, to venture an opinion on the vexed question as to why so many have a leaning towards the seamy and sinister side of life, we should be

disposed to consider that, apart from the allure-
ment of the abnormal and the inclination to indulge a morbid curiosity, perhaps the chief influence
serving to stimulate the mind of the public when a
great crime has been perpetrated is a genuine concern that a serious outrage has been made on society,
constituting a veritable menace to its security.

We have stated in a former chapter that Curtius,
more than a century ago, had allocated a part of
his Museum in Paris to models of men of ill-repute,
and had named it the "Caverne des Grands
Voleurs." How far this place approximated to
the present Chamber of Horrors we cannot say, but
it certainly must have created a precedent for the
placing of the portraits and the relics of law-
breakers in a place separate and apart from the
main and more reputable portion of the Exhibition.

In 1802, when Madame Tussaud crossed the
Channel to establish her Exhibition permanently
in this country, she did not, in all probability, find
it easy to obtain an additional room for these
figures, especially when touring through the pro-
vinces. Nevertheless, when she had to exhibit her
models in the same hall, she undoubtedly differ-
entiated, to the best of her ability, between the
famous and the infamous by grouping the models
of evil-doers in a corner by themselves.

When the Exhibition was opened in Baker Street,
the Chamber of Horrors became a recognised feature
of the collection. It was at first called the " Dead

Room," although some designated it the "Black Room," owing to its sombre aspect.

Its chief exhibit at that time was the guillotine, surrounded by the impressions of heads that had been decapitated by it. Here also was shown the model of Marat dying in his bath, besides many other relics of the Revolution. Indeed, it might have been regarded as the nucleus of an historical museum dealing exclusively with the last days of the old French Monarchy. Even the walls were constructed and draped in imitation of the interior of the Bastille, the principal keys of which were shown therein as mementoes of unusual interest.

" Mr. Punch " made his début before the British public somewhere during the early forties, and, as already indicated, he took an early opportunity of referring to this part of the Tussaud collection as the " Chamber of Horrors," by which title it has been known ever since.

The number of persons visiting this extra room during these days was not great, except on those occasions when the business was galvanised into activity by the addition of a portrait-model of some unworthy being who happened for the nonce to figure largely in the public eye.

There came into our possession at a time beyond my memory a singular and valuable sketch, by Sir Thomas Lawrence, of the alleged murderer, Williams, as he appeared directly after he had hanged himself in Coldbath Fields prison.

Williams was accused of the murders of the Marr and the Williamson families in the East End of London under peculiarly brutal circumstances. These massacres, which were committed in December, 1811, caused an immense sensation, and inspired the remarkable monograph of de Quincey entitled *Murder as One of the Fine Arts*.

How Lawrence came to make such a drawing, and what induced so refined and dignified a person to interest himself in a subject so repulsive, it is difficult to understand. Although Lawrence had not then been elected to the presidency of the Royal Academy, he held a high position in society as the first portrait painter of his day.

We give an illustration of the sketch in question which is quite authentic.

Until 1823 it was directed that the body of a suicide should be buried in a cross-road and have a stake driven through it, and there can be little doubt that that of Williams was thus treated. It was not, indeed, until 1882 that an Act was passed putting an end to this barbarous custom.

This circumstance readily calls to mind Tom Hood's description of the fate that befell Ben Battle, the victim of Faithless Nelly Gray :

> A dozen men sat on his corpse,
>   To find out why he died—
> And they buried Ben in four cross-roads,
>   With a *stake* in his inside !

JOHN WILLIAMS
after he had committed suicide in prison.

(*From a drawing by Sir Thomas Lawrence, P.R.A.*)

[To face p. 252.

Of the characters that became, in course of time, suitable objects for the "Dead Room" we have neither the space nor the inclination to dwell upon, but a passing reference to two or three that helped to give the place its present distinctiveness may prove interesting.

The hideous crimes perpetrated by Burke and Hare, to which slight reference has already been made, took place about the year 1828, and the memory of those crimes was still fresh in the mind of the public when we opened in Baker Street; indeed, a matter of six years could not suffice for its obliteration.

The appalling revelation that it was not only possible, but easy, for one's neighbour to be decoyed away, put to death, and his body sold, without question, for a sum varying from £8 to £14, aroused a feeling of consternation throughout the country of a very real and lasting character.

The high prices paid for bodies required for dissection had begotten this terrible traffic. At least sixteen murders had been traced to these miscreants, but the evidence at the trial failed to answer the question " How many more ? "

Burke was executed in January, 1829, on the strength of Hare's evidence, so that for nearly a century have the portrait-models of these two notorious criminals stood facing each other. There are to this day many visitors who, on catching sight of their forbidding features, seem to recognise them, and make ready comment, without the aid of a Catalogue, on the leading circumstances associated with their nefarious careers.

The very first startling event that furnished a subject for the " Dead Room," when the Exhibition opened in Baker Street in 1835, was the attempt on the life of Louis Philippe, King of the French, four months later.

It had been the custom of His Majesty to review the Gardes Nationales and the garrison of Paris on each anniversary of the Revolution of 1830. For some considerable time the King and his Government had been growing very unpopular, and many warnings had been given him to desist from this military function ; but, in spite of all advice, he persisted in holding the review.

The anniversary of the Revolution was on the 28th of July, and the King, followed by a numerous Staff, left the Tuileries at half-past ten on the morning of that day, accompanied by his three sons, the Ducs d'Orléans, de Nemour, and de Joinville.

In passing along the Boulevard du Temple— and, strange to say, when almost opposite the site of Curtius's old Museum—a noise was heard resembling an irregular musket fire. In an instant the road and pavement at the point where Louis had been riding was strewn with dead and dying men and horses, and amid the mêlée the King, slightly wounded in the forehead, stood alone by the side of his injured horse.

More than forty persons had been struck and nineteen killed or mortally wounded.   Among the latter was Edward Joseph Mortier, Duc de Trevise, the famous Marshal of Napoleon I.

After a few moments' suspense, attention was directed to a cloud of smoke issuing from the third-floor window of a house on the Boulevard.   Herein was discovered a machine composed of a row of twenty-five gun-barrels so arranged as to cover the cavalcade as it passed the premises.   It had been fired by a train of gunpowder, with the result that several of the barrels had burst on the discharge.

The room was empty, but from one of the back windows of the house the police caught sight of a man huddled up in a corner of the courtyard below. He was trying to stanch the blood which was flowing from a great wound in his head.   In spite of his injury, caused by his firing of the infernal machine, he had had the strength to stagger out of the room, seize a rope, secure it to a window, and by its means escape from the house.

The man turned out to be Giuseppe Fieschi, a rabid conspirator.   Our model of him was added some weeks after the event, and, being placed by the side of an exact copy of the machine he had used, the man and his diabolical contrivance proved of considerable interest, a circumstance that substantially assisted to establish the Exhibition as a permanent London attraction.

This political crime was, however, soon eclipsed by one of a particularly sordid character committed much nearer home.

James Greenacre who murdered his fiancée, Hannah Brown, by striking her a fatal blow in a fit of temper, will ever figure as a criminal of a very curious type. Many a deed like that which brought him to the scaffold has occasioned but a passing interest. It was the means he adopted for the purpose of evading the consequences of his crime that aroused the excitement and indignation of the people. He dismembered the body, and deliberately distributed it in broad daylight to widely different parts of the Metropolis.

The discovery of the various parts of the body from time to time, the bringing of them together, and the final identification of the remains wrought up the public mind to a state of high tension, and after the culprit had been brought to justice many thousands visited the Exhibition to scan for themselves the features of his model which had been installed.

It will be remembered that we are dealing with a period when the extreme penalty of the law was exacted in public, a condition of things which lasted till 1868, when it was enacted that all executions should take place privately within prison walls.

The night before Greenacre's execution at Newgate (the 2nd of May, 1837) hundreds slept on the prison steps and round about the neighbourhood of the old gaol. Crowds spent the night in taverns and lodging-houses, indulging in unseemly revelry and ribald and drunken dissipation. Nor were the spectators all drawn from the lowest class ; all classes were represented. Positions within sight of the drop fetched from five shillings to a couple of guineas each, and a first-floor room overlooking the scaffold commanded as much as £12, no small price in those days.

It is a grim story, but who has not been entertained by the account in the *Ingoldsby Legends* of the way in which "My Lord Tomnoddy" failed to witness the launching into eternity of a doomed fellow creature ?

As the result of a happy thought from " Tiger Tim "—

" An't please you, my Lord, there's a man to be hang'd "—

Tomnoddy invites a party of convivial friends to enjoy the scene, for

> " To see a man swing
> At the end of a string,
> With his neck in a noose, will be quite a new thing."

So he

> Turns down the Old Bailey,
> Where, in front of the gaol, he
> Pulls up at the door of the gin-shop, and gaily
> Cries, " What must I fork out to-night, my trump,
> For the whole first-floor of the Magpie and Stump ? "

S

St. Sepulchre's clock strikes eight, and

> God ! 'tis a fearsome thing to see
> That pale wan man's mute agony,—
> The glare of that wild, despairing eye,
> Now bent on the crowd, now turn'd to the sky.

. . . . . .

> Oh ! 'twas a fearsome sight ! Ah me !
> A deed to shudder at,—not to see.

The clock strikes

> Nine ! 'twas the last concluding stroke !
> And then—my Lord Tomnoddy awoke !

. . . .

> " Hollo ! Hollo !
> Here's a rum go !
> Why, Captain !—my Lord !—here's the devil to pay !
> The fellow's been cut down and taken away !
> What's to be done ?
> We've missed all the fun ! "

. . . . . .

> What *was* to be done ? The man was dead !
> Nought *could* be done—nought could be said ;
> So—my Lord Tomnoddy went home to bed !

Referring back to the days before the advent
of the daily illustrated papers with their portraits
of all kinds of people, a very affecting story
was once told by a well-known author.

It related to a very pretty and plaintive young
woman who visited the Chamber of Horrors early
on the morning that a certain criminal with many
aliases was executed.

She was accompanied by her father, who, with
his arm about her waist to steady her faltering

steps, led her up to where the figure of the murderer stood. The poor woman remained gazing at it as though fascinated ; then, with a nod, she burst out crying and buried her head in her hands.

Her father gently drew her out of the place, and as he did so whispered in her ear, " Free, my child ; free at last ! "

How the author came to hear of the incident we do not know, or was it one of those coincidences that somehow do occur ?

CHAPTER XLII

WE have speculated much upon the origin of what has come to be called "The Chamber of Horrors Rumour," relating to a popular delusion that Madame Tussaud's will pay a sum of money to any person who spends a night alone with the criminals assembled therein.

It need hardly be pointed out that no such ridiculous challenge was ever issued to the public, although the rumour has run for nearly twenty years, in spite of repeated contradictions.

I am not even hopeful that what I am writing now will produce the desired result of disabusing adventurous minds of this impression ; in fact, denials on our part appear rather to have tended to give wider currency to the rumour. Thousands of letters have been received from volunteers of both sexes eager and anxious to undertake the ordeal for rewards which vary, in their imaginations, from £5 to £5,000.

Among the aspirants have been soldiers, sailors,

ex-policemen, and even domestic servants, all of whom insisted that their nerves were equal to the task. Only the other day I received a letter from a Scotsman who intimated his willingness to forgo any pecuniary reward if only we would furnish him with a bottle of whisky and some sandwiches with which to regale himself as he sat at the feet of Burke and Hare.

The conclusion has somehow taken possession of our minds that this fallacious rumour emanated, innocently enough, from a story told long ago by one "Dagonet" of a man who was said to have been accidentally locked all night in the Chamber. Originally, I imagine, people must have offered voluntarily to spend a night there for a consideration, and then, as the subject came to be talked about, it very easily grew into the form of a challenge said to have been made by us, which, of course, was never made and never will be made.

Considerable fillip was given to the rumour by the Chamber of Horrors scene in *The Whip* at Drury Lane Theatre in 1909.

From some source or another handbills in the following form were plentifully distributed :

£100 REWARD

will be given to any person, male or female, who will pass the night alone in the Chamber of Horrors at Madame Tussaud's Exhibition. The only condition made is that the daring one shall not smoke or drink or read during the twelve hours he passes with the wax figures of the world's noted criminals.

It was also stated on the handbill that the above was a copy of a placard said to have been issued many years ago, but, in spite of the large reward, no one came forward to try the experiment, and that now, after many years, " Tom Lambert, the trainer of The Whip, undergoes this horrible experience in the Drury Lane drama."

So far so good, for dramatic purposes—and that is all.

Apparently it was something of this sort that the bard had in mind who wrote the following stanza :

> I dreamt that I slept at Madame Tussaud's
> With cut-throats and kings by my side,
> And that all the wax figures in those weird abodes
> At midnight became vivified.

Until the recent escapade of a venturesome young lady, the only instance I can recall of any person spending the night alone in the Chamber of Horrors falls accidentally to the credit of a policeman on duty at the Exhibition when the opening of the present building was celebrated in July, 1884. A reception was then held which lasted until after midnight, and naturally it became necessary that the place should be guarded till the return of the staff in the morning.

The policeman in question was put in charge of the criminals in the Chamber of Horrors, with liberty to relieve the monotony of his eerie vigil by strolling through the other parts of the building, which included access to the room in which the refreshments had been served. Wines and spirits and other good things were left nominally under his care—whereby hangs a tale.

When the time came to relieve the policeman in the morning, he could not be found, and after a long search an Exhibition attendant heard the sound of moaning proceeding from one of the docks in the Chamber of Horrors. Here lay asleep the missing police-officer, in a condition that pointed to the probability of his having had recourse to the wines of the feast, presumably as a means of fortifying his courage.

The incident caused some little concern, but the officer's position was so well understood and the extenuating circumstances were so obvious that his misadventure came to be jocularly treated as an excusable lapse. He had not only spent the night in the dread abode of criminals, but had actually slept there—a much more surprising performance.

Yet another reminiscence of the Chamber of Horrors, just a little creepy.

Sauntering one night through its gloomy passages after the last visitor had departed and the watchmen, having passed me on their rounds, had lowered the lights to a feeble glimmer, my attention was drawn in some unaccountable way towards one of the models.

" I could swear that figure moved," I said to myself. " But no, the notion is too ridiculous."

I looked at it again, carefully this time. I was

not mistaken. The figure *did* move, and, what was more, it moved distinctly towards me. It appeared to bend slowly forward, as though in preparation for a sudden bound, and I thought it looked at me with a fixed and malignant stare.

Just as I was expecting it to raise its arms and seize me by the throat, it stopped dead, and remained at a grotesque and ludicrous angle, apparently looking for something on the floor.

What was the explanation of this thrilling experience?

The vibration caused by a heavy goods train on the Metropolitan Railway, which runs under the Exhibition premises, had shaken the figure off its balance, and the iron which fastened it to the floor permitted it to move and lean forward in the uncanny manner I have described.

The following comedy of the Chamber of Horrors from which the chief actor derived a minimum of amusement, if any, comes into my mind as having been described by the elder Dumas, and is calculated to relieve the gloom that is naturally associated with the place:

" A young Parisian, visiting the Exhibition in London, found himself temporarily alone in the famous Chamber, and was seized with the ambition of being able to say, on his return to his favourite Paris café, that his neck had been held in the same lunette which had once encircled those of Louis XVI. and Marie Antoinette.

" The idea was no sooner conceived than carried out, and for quite five minutes the rash young man enjoyed his novel position under the knife of the very same guillotine which had once worked such havoc among the aristocrats in the gay city.

"When, however, he was about to touch the spring that would release him, a thought struck him which threw him into a cold sweat.

" Supposing he were to touch the wrong spring, might not the knife come down, with the result not only of beheading him, but of making the world believe a most sensational suicide had been committed?

" He shouted for help, and at length an attendant, followed by a crowd of visitors, appeared.

" 'What is the matter?' they asked in English; but the official was equal to the occasion, and turned it to good account.

" 'À l'aide! Au secours!' yelled the Parisian, who could only speak French.

" 'A little patience,' answered the other.

" 'What does he say?' was the general query.

" 'Oh, it's a part of his performance, ladies and gentlemen. You see, Madame Tussaud is not satisfied with merely exhibiting the guillotine. She wishes to show you how it is actually worked.'

" This statement was greeted with general applause by everybody except the victim, who continued entreating to be released, whilst the impromptu lecturer calmly explained to the audience the practical working of the death-dealing machine.

" ' Bravo ! How well he acts ! ' was the verdict, as the prisoner appealed frantically in a language which none else but the attendant understood.

" Finally, on being at last released, he fainted. They brought him round with smelling-salts and cold water, and the first thing he did was to feel if his head was still safe. Satisfied on this point, he fled, without stopping to find his hat, and lost not an instant in starting at once for Paris."

I come now, by a sudden transition, to write of three notable shrieval servants whose occupation, however indispensable, was unsavoury.

Calcraft, the first to be styled the " Yeoman of the Halter," I had not the " pleasure " of knowing.

We have the original signboard he used to exhibit outside his house. It is a framed piece of wood, about three feet by two feet, and it bears in black letters the following notice :

J. CALCRAFT,

Boot and Shoe Maker,

Executioner to Her Majesty.

His successor, Marwood, sat on several occasions for his model.

The executioner would sometimes visit the studios when his spirits were low, and a pipe and a glass of gin and water—his favourite beverage—were always at his service.

Then he would go down to the Chamber of Horrors to see some of his old acquaintances around whose necks he had so delicately adjusted the fatal noose. He would stop before each one with a grim look, while his lips moved tremulously.

" Put me there," he once said after he had given a sitting.

It was like a man choosing the site of his grave.

His companion on these visits was a grizzled terrier. One day he came alone.

" Your dog, Mr. Marwood—where is it ? " he was asked.

The old man was sad.

"My poor old dog is dying—my dog that knew the business like a Christian and the inside of every prison in England ; that has played with my ropes ; that has caught rats in my business bags."

" Dying by inches," was the unfeeling rejoinder of a bystander, followed by the cruel suggestion, " Why don't you hang him ? "

Marwood gave him a reproachful glance.

" No, no. Hang a man, but my dear old dog— never ! "

Poor Marwood had a good heart, and the story of the dog was so affecting that the interview abruptly terminated.

Berry, the executioner, was paid for a sitting, and seemed by no means averse from having his figure placed in the Chamber of Horrors, where it may now be seen. He rather appeared to be proud of his official calling.

CHAPTER XLIII

As I proceed with my narrative, having already
travelled through the memories of many years, there
seem to crowd at my heels, so to speak, a great collection of humorous and curious incidents which,
although unrelated to each other, are yet worthy of
a place in this chronicle.

They come of their own free will readily enough
when I want to engage in serious work, but no
amount of persuasion will lure them from their lurk-
ing-places when I want to recount them. As I fancy
my friends like my short stories as well as any, I
propose to introduce a few trivialities that are
sufficiently obliging to present themselves as I write.

In the Berlin Treaty days a staunchly Conservative
borough was celebrating the event, and among other
decorations was a large transparency showing Lord
Beaconsfield and Lord Salisbury standing together,
with the motto " Peace with Honour" beneath them.
An old woman went up to the borough M.P. and
asked :

" If you please, sir, will you tell me which is Peace ? "

Charles Peace was the man of the moment just then.

Mark Twain, according to his cousin, Katherine Clemens, once visited Madame Tussaud's. He stood a long while, says his cousin, in contemplation of an especially clever piece of work, and was aroused by a sudden stab of pain in his side. Turning quickly, he found himself face to face with a dumb-founded British matron with her parasol still pointed at him.

" O lor', it's alive ! " she exclaimed, and beat a hasty retreat.

The best known of all cricketers, Dr. W. G. Grace, has long enjoyed a well-earned place of prominence in the Exhibition, and even to-day, when the great master of the bat and the ball is no longer with us, his portrait continues to attract more than an average share of attention.

Dr. Grace was very fond of telling the following story about a trusted old servant of his whom he treated on one occasion to a trip to London. On her return he asked her what it was that pleased her most among the sights of the Metropolis.

" Oh, sir, Madame Tussaud's was beautiful," replied Susan.

" Then you must have seen me there ? " said her master.

" No, that I did not, sir."

" What ! How did you miss me ? I am there as large as life."

" Well, sir, to tell you the truth, it cost sixpence extra to go into the Chamber of Horrors."

A young girl arriving at an institution at Torquay, from London, was asked whether she had ever visited Westminster Abbey. She hesitated, and was then reminded that that historic edifice contained monuments of the Kings and Queens of England. She immediately brightened up, and replied, " Oh, yes, I have been there, but they call it Madame Tussaud's now."

A short time after the seated figure of Mr. Rudyard Kipling, which is still to be seen in the Exhibition, had been modelled, the following conversation is reported to have occurred between a young lady and her maid, who had visited Madame Tussaud's :

Relating her experiences there, the girl remarked :

" They've got Mr. Kipling and another murderer there, miss."

" But Mr. Kipling isn't a murderer," said her young mistress.

" No, miss," was the reply, " but they've got him there, miss."

During those days when the Exhibition was being removed from one town to another the figures of criminals originally stood together in the same room with all the other models ; but as it was suggested that it was indecorous to have the effigies of criminals in such close proximity with those of illustrious personages, Madame Tussaud had the former removed to a separate room, and the Chamber of Horrors was formed as it now exists.

The relatives and friends of criminals frequently visit the Chamber.

At a drawing-room meeting held at the residence of Lady Esther Smith, in Grosvenor Place, in aid of the Social Institutes' Union, which exists to provide facilities for establishing clubs on temperance lines, Mrs. (now Lady) Bland-Sutton told the story of a little girl who was asked where she would like to go for a treat.

" To Madame Tussaud's," was the prompt reply.

" But you went there last year," it was objected.

" Oh, yes, I know," said the child, " but father wasn't in the Chamber of Horrors then."

Somewhat similar is the following :

A parlourmaid, interviewed by her mistress just after a Bank Holiday, was asked :

" And how did you spend your day off, Polly ? "

"Oh, we went to Madame Tussaud's," was the reply. " We always go there, mum. You see, having uncle in the Chamber of Horrors gives the place a family interest, so to speak."

When Dr. Jackson was Bishop of London he gave a breakfast to several curates before they left to take up missionary work abroad, and one of them, in the course of conversation at the repast, observed that he had just visited Madame Tussaud's, where he had heard a figure of his Grace had been on view for many years.

He said he much regretted that he could not find the figure anywhere in the Exhibition, although he had searched for it high and low.

" Oh," said the Bishop, " haven't you heard, my dear boy, that they've melted me down for Peace ? " —a sally that was greeted with roars of laughter.

Many complaints have been made by foreigners visiting London regarding the inefficiency of guides with little or no knowledge of the places with which they are supposed to be thoroughly acquainted.

For instance, a certain Teuton of great pretensions brought to Madame Tussaud's a party of travellers from a Prussian provincial town, and informed them, among other things, that Mrs. Maybrick, whose model was then in the Napoleon Rooms, was a lady connected with the life of the great Bonaparte.

CHAPTER XLIV

WE now come to the eventful period that began in
August, 1914.

At the beginning of hostilities the Kaiser, Count
Zeppelin, and other German objectionables were
relegated to a less conspicuous position than they
had formerly occupied. The enemy had not at that
time gained the animosity which his subsequent
acts of " frightfulness " earned for him, but he soon
showed himself in his true colours.

It was in the spring of 1910 that a renewed portrait of the German Emperor had been given a place
of honour, with the Empress by his side, near our
own royal group. Not very long afterwards the
British public began to suspect the Kaiser of evil
designs upon this country, and visitors frequently
indicated their displeasure in front of his model.

With the outbreak of war, naturally enough, came
an outburst of general reprobation, and the atro-
cities committed by the German Army and Navy
provoked impulsive patriots to visible and audible

T

manifestations of anger. More than once the Kaiser had his figure struck by men, while women shook their fists and umbrellas in the face of the world's greatest homicide.

As a matter of fact, to the Kaiser belongs the distinction of having been expelled from Madame Tussaud's for several months—a distinction that was shared by the late Francis Joseph, Emperor of Austria.

This was done in deference to public opinion, which had become very hostile to their models being shown at Madame Tussaud's. Letters had appeared to this effect in the Press, and one periodical published a large cartoon showing the Kaiser and his associates in the prisoners' dock in the Chamber of Horrors.

Originally four enemy monarchs had pedestals in an obscure corner of Room No. 4. They were the Kaiser, the late Emperor of Austria, the Sultan of Turkey, and King Ferdinand of Bulgaria.

The Sultan of Turkey, as an unkind friend remarked, " found his level in the melting-pot " some time ago ; and the Kaiser twice had to undergo a surgical operation as the result of bouts with ultra-patriotic visitors. Ferdinand of Bulgaria also had some narrow escapes, especially from our " handymen," who have a short way with all enemies.

Some time ago my attention was called to the fact that one of the " spikes " of the Kaiser's moustache had been clipped off, giving him a ludicrously woe-begone appearance. I have always suspected the Colonials of that " cut," and if I am wrong—well, I apologise. Perhaps the " spike " will be heard of some other day as a souvenir of the war.

Feeling ran so high after the sinking of the *Lusitania* that we readily yielded to the public demand, and evicted the Huns from the house.

On the 16th of September, 1916, *John Bull* had addressed to us the following open letter on the subject of the presence of the objectionable figures :

To the Directors, Madame Tussaud & Sons, Ltd.,
Baker Street, W.

GENTLEMEN,

Being an admirer of your Moral Waxworks, I am sure you will excuse me if I indicate a blot upon your interesting and intellectual display. As a matter of fact, there are four blots.

They occur in your Grand Hall, No. 4, and they take the form of effigies representing, with a fidelity almost lifelike, those malodorous monarchs the Sultan of Turkey, King Ferdinand of Bulgaria, the Emperor of Austria, and that arch-villain Kaiser Bill.

Do, please, reshuffle the pack, gentlemen. Take the sinful quartette out of your Grand Hall, which they desecrate, and place them in that other room of yours which seems specially designed for their accommodation—the Chamber of Horrors.

In the company of Burke and Hare, Charles Peace, Greenacre, and Wainwright, they will be quite at home.

JOHN BULL.

John Bull on the 14th of November printed the following, containing my reply :

BRAVO, TUSSAUD !

PATRIOTIC ACTION OF THE GREAT EXHIBITION.

We have received the following interesting letter from Mr. J. T. Tussaud :

" As a regular reader of your valuable and most instructive paper, my attention was drawn to your letter, addressed to my company, which appeared in your issue of the 16th September.

" In it you call attention to what you describe as a blot—or rather four blots—upon ' our interesting and intellectual display,' namely, the inclusion of the Sultan of Turkey, the King of Bulgaria, and the Emperors of Austria and Germany in our collection of celebrities and notorieties. Of course, such a letter from such an influential person could not pass unnoticed, and it was brought before my Board of Directors at the earliest opportunity.

" Prior to the date of your letter the pack had already been reshuffled, and the figures to which you refer had been relegated to a much less conspicuous position than they had previously occupied. When your letter was penned they were conspiring against the peace of Europe in a small room which contains the tableau representing ' The Destruction of Messina '—a scene of ruin which seems to be in keeping with this Machiavellian group.

" Like yourself, other visitors had frequently suggested that the quartette should be placed in another famous —or infamous—part of the Exhibition ; but the trouble was that Burke and Hare, Charles Peace, Greenacre, and Wainwright, whom you name, and their comparatively innocuous companions, would not hear of their abode being thus desecrated.

" What were we to do ?

" I am now pleased to inform you that after considering your remarks a solution has been arrived at : the pack has been shuffled again, and, by a remarkable feat of legerdemain, the four knaves have now disappeared altogether."

We congratulate Messrs. Tussaud on this happy solution to the problem.

The restoration of two of the figures was due to a very singular circumstance. Our overseas soldiers soon began to visit Madame Tussaud's in large numbers, and they frequently expressed disappointment at not being able to see the two enemy Emperors whose armies they had come so far to fight.

Sympathising with their point of view, we had the Kaiser and Francis Joseph readmitted, placing them in an isolated position, with the "All-Highest" at one time confronting the Messina tableau, and more recently faced by the tableau of the Ruhleben horse-box in which British prisoners had to spend four long weary years of separation from home and family. In the same room are models of Prince Bismarck and Count von Moltke.

It was some little time after the Kaiser's reinstatement that a British sailor, who was quite unable to control his feelings, after glowering for several minutes at the figure, made a run at it and knocked it over. The head was smashed and the figure badly damaged.

The tar's friends, who were much concerned at their companion's escapade, strove to pacify him, and contrived to get him out of the building without further trouble ; but the Kaiser had to go into hospital for repairs.

The sailor was carried away by an impulse thousands have with difficulty controlled out of respect for the Exhibition and the law which makes it an offence to destroy other people's property.

Two days after the incident a little boy inquired of an Exhibition attendant where he could see the pieces of the Kaiser, as he would like to take a bit away.

A party of twenty-eight American soldiers happened to be passing the curtained room where the dismembered model of the Kaiser lay, and one of them made the request that they should be shown the " All-Highest " lying in state.

" And a very bad state, too," replied the attendant, who could not oblige.

The second serious attack upon the Kaiser's effigy took place two or three months after the first.

On this occasion it was a Colonial soldier who, seeing the restored monarch gazing at him in a supercilious fashion, as he imagined, drew from its scabbard the sword of the defunct Austrian Emperor, whose model sits close by, and stabbed the Kaiser's figure in the face.

The force with which the thrust was delivered was such that off came the monarch's head, and again the model had to be taken to hospital for the surgical operation of restoring the head and refixing it to its trunk.

Count Zeppelin, whose name will for ever be associated with the introduction of aerial warships and the dropping of bombs upon defenceless people, has had many a clenched fist shaken at him standing there beside the portraits of Roger Casement and Tribich Lincoln.

Though never actually assaulted, it was only the stolidity of the British character that kept people's hands off his effigy during the Zeppelin raids on London. Visitors were too proud, I suppose, to touch him, and from the time the first German airship was brought down in flames on British soil Count Zeppelin's model began to be ignored.

A British matron quietly remarked, as she stopped an instant in front of the portrait, " So you're going the way of all our enemies—beaten at your own game."

In the early months of the war we borrowed from a soldier an Iron Cross that he had taken from the breast of a dead German officer whom he had found lying in a wood at Zillebeke, near Ypres, in November, 1914.

According to the story of the soldier—Drummer Newman, of the Grenadier Guards—our men, comprising Grenadier Guards, Irish Guards, and Oxfordshire Light Infantry, were opposed to the Prussian Guards, who were driven out of the wood, leaving behind them several hundreds of their dead.

Newman was searching for dispatches when he happened upon the cross in question. I remember him coming to my studio with the trophy. He was a typical soldier, and he greatly amused me by his description of the way in which old soldiers —bearing in mind one of the trite sayings of Frederick the Great—would hearten their comrades, saying, just before going over the top, " Now then, boys, you don't want to live for ever, do you ? "

The Iron Cross was exhibited with other relics, and used to be handed round for inspection, until one day it was missing. That was in October, 1915, and, although we made inquiries of the police and learned that it had been seen in the neighbourhood of the Exhibition, we heard no more of it till, several months later, it was traced by detectives to a gentleman at Warrington who had innocently purchased it from an invalided soldier.

We willingly refunded the amount that had been paid for the cross, and it has now been restored to our collection.

No sooner was London subjected to the terrible ordeal of air-raids than we received, as was only to be expected, offers of bombs that had been dropped by enemy aircraft.

As a matter of fact, we acquired one of the first of these missiles, and it proved of great interest to our visitors, especially to our own airmen, who never tired of describing to their friends the construction of the bomb and the way in which it was dropped.

We found it necessary, however, to discourage the bringing of ammunition to the Exhibition, as we had no desire that the building should be wrecked by the untimely explosion of a live bomb or shell.

Reverting for a moment to the attacks upon the effigy of the ex-Kaiser, I am reminded of one or two occasions when figures have incurred the animosity of beholders, although not to the same extent.

A professional rider, expelled from the Jockey Club, used to visit the Exhibition very often for the sole purpose of venting his spleen against the image of his supposed enemy, Fred Archer, the jockey who won five Derbys ; and he was heard to remark that it was " so like the beggar, I would give anything to smash it."

In August, 1893, an old man, whose whole get-up spoke of better days, was seen to walk up to the effigy of the late Jabez Spencer Balfour, shake his withered, palsied fist in its face, and totter out of the building.

CHAPTER XLV

Tussaud's during the war—Chameleon crowds—The psychology
of courage—Men of St. Dunstan's—Poignant memories—
Our watchman's soliloquy.

UNDER the stress of war many strange things revealed themselves at Tussaud's—things by no
means easy to define, subtle, illusive, immaterial,
difficult to comprehend and hard to describe.

At the outbreak of hostilities the attendance
suffered a severe check. This disquieting effect
was in the main, I believe, due to the great wrench
suffered by the public mind through the country's
sudden transition from the normal condition of
peace to a strenuous state of war. But as each
month passed the flow of visitors steadily increased
in volume, until it far exceeded that of pre-war
days.

By the time the manhood of the Empire had,
in a great measure, doffed its sombre everyday
suit and donned khaki, khaki became the dominant
colour of the throng that filled the Exhibition
rooms.

With this change in attire there came a
marked alteration in its demeanour. Usually sedate

and reserved, it now betrayed—in startling contradiction to all reasonable expectations—a cheery, devil-me-care character which, curious to relate, resolved itself into a tone unmistakably flippant ; a mental attitude to which we soon realised we must give our careful consideration.

He would indeed have been a poor psychologist who had taken this outward showing as a true indication of the feelings of our brave fellows ; for it was obviously but the assumption of that demeanour so strongly characteristic of the British disposition, that of facing an ugly job in a cheerful spirit.

It was the ready answer to the pessimist, " If it's got to be done, what's the use of being miserable about it ? "—a philosophical bearing that perhaps found its deepest expression in their " Cheerio ! " and insouciant wave of the hand bidding farewell to wife, mother, and child ere turning to face the grim realities and dread uncertainty of war.

To keep pace with the stirring and ever-fluctuating events of the day, large maps of the battle areas were specially produced for the Exhibition, and lectures were given before them, explaining our varying fortunes in the great conflict. It was in the giving of these lectures that we were soon able to take a fairly correct measure of the disposition of our visitors.

They were, first of all, delivered on somewhat

academic lines, with, perhaps, too pronounced an idea of imparting instruction rather than that of affording entertainment. It was soon found that if the attention of our visitors was to be held, it was necessary to adopt a more optimistic and lively, if not an almost bantering, tone if the dissertation were to receive any real mark of appreciation on the part of those who cared to listen.

As the struggle proceeded Tussaud's began to assume the position of a *pointe de réunion* of a very remarkable character, and this quite irrespective of class or nationality.

We opened our doors as early as eight o'clock in the morning, and even then found that not a few had been waiting for admission for some considerable time. This forced upon us the conviction that the Exhibition had risen in favour as something of a place of refuge by those who had involuntarily found themselves abroad early in the morning and had borne its existence in mind.

Be this as it may, throughout all hours of the day Tussaud's proved a centre of attraction to many champions of their country's cause. Here they were to be seen, whether on their final leave before going out to the front, or homeward bound to enjoy a brief respite from the turmoil of the conflict, and awaiting a train to carry them to their families.

During the autumn of 1914 and far into the

following year there congregated within our walls
numerous hapless and pathetic beings, strangers
to us by their foreign tongue, who, having come
from nowhere in particular and having nowhere in
particular to go, aimlessly wandered into the
Exhibition.

We can only presume that they came to help
pass away many a sad and anxious hour, or
maybe to take measure of the semblance of
those who were at that very moment foremost
in striving to stem the tide of the cruel incursion
that had driven them to take refuge in a foreign
land.

Then as time wore on there came a touch of re-
lieving colour that showed itself here and there
amid the prevailing khaki ; at first a mere fleck that
gradually became more pronounced as the war
advanced. This was the hospital blue of our
valiant soldiers who had not passed unscathed
through the ordeal of fire, as cheery a gathering
as ever set foot within the place, a cheeriness
readily responded to by their fellow visitors through
the medium of sympathy and admiration.

One sad sight there was, however, which touched
the hearts of the people so deeply that no display
of cheerfulness on the part of the sufferers—and
they, too, were invariably light-hearted—could
quite evoke a sense of mirth.

St. Dunstan's Hostel for Blinded Soldiers and Sailors
in Regent's Park is not very far from Madame

Tussaud's, and many of its inmates visited the Exhibition, and, for the matter of that, still find a pleasure in coming in couples or small parties to spend an hour or so among the models and the relics.

In spite of the distressing fact that they have been deprived of the gift of sight, they stand in front of the models and pause while the biographies are read out to them from the Catalogue by some more fortunate companion. Then they almost invariably nod to express their comprehension of the subject before them, and seem to see and understand through the faculty of their imagination much that would otherwise have been made manifest to them through the function of their eyes.

During the past few years our attendance has totalled to a figure reaching several millions; but the number visiting the place hardly constitutes so remarkable a fact as the many diverse nationalities and tribes they represented, or their coming from so many far-distant and remote parts of the world.

The landing of a fresh contingent at any one of our ports, or the arrival in London of any body of men attached to our Allied Forces, brought distinct and unfamiliar types of humanity to our doors.

"I had often heard of the place, but never thought I should have had an opportunity of seeing it," was a remark that often fell upon the ears of our attendants; and we know, for many reasons, that most of them had made up their minds to visit the place long before they had set foot upon our shores.

Of the many telling experiences of the last few momentous years, the one that will be retained longest in our memory will most assuredly be the touching sight of the war-stained and weary men who, during the earlier days of the war, literally stumbled through our turnstiles into the building.

Dazed for want of sleep, begrimed and besmeared with the very mud of the trenches, they flung themselves upon the nearest ottoman or couch, or in some out-of-the-way place upon the floor, to snatch a few hours' sleep in comparative comfort.

One evening, when strolling round the rooms some time after the place had been closed, I found myself looking at the watchmen, who were busily engaged sweeping the floors. The chief among them, an old and valued servant, possessing a disposition that generally enabled him to look upon the bright side of things—although he was so often constrained to view them only during the sombre hours of the night —caught me gazing at him.

With a face I thought unusually grave he bade me " Good-evening," and ruefully remarked, " It seems to me, sir, some of this dirt has come a long way." Then, pondering for a while, with his eyes fixed upon the floor, he resumed, " Yes, sir, some of it from the very trenches." And I somehow believed the old fellow was right.

CHAPTER XLVI

THERE are three figures, added during the past few momentous years, which possess the rare distinction of being models of abiding interest. Out of the many portraits placed in the Exhibition, there are few that stay there very long.

Nurse Cavell, Jack Cornwell, and Captain Fryatt will always be remembered with esteem by the present generation, and the great story of their heroic deeds ensures for them a permanent home at Baker Street, where they will be viewed with patriotic pride by posterity. The portrait of Edith Cavell, the martyr-nurse, was modelled immediately after that heroic woman was brutally shot by the Germans at Brussels at two o'clock in the morning of Tuesday, the 12th of October, 1915.

I communicated with the London Hospital, Whitechapel, where Nurse Cavell had served before she went to Belgium, and the nurses there readily afforded me all the information they had to impart.

Several of them visited my studio and gave me valuable hints as to the posing of the figure and the general demeanour of Miss Cavell when at the hospital. They particularly described the way in which she used to walk through the wards with a book under her arm and her head inclined slightly to one side. When the model was finished they were good enough to say that it enabled them to visualise Miss Cavell as they knew her, and that it was a pleasing portrait.

My wife prepared the laurel wreath, placed above the model, on which are inscribed Nurse Cavell's words, uttered a few hours before her death, " I am happy to die for my country."

Soon after the boy hero of the Jutland naval battle was modelled and he had been awarded the posthumous honour of the Victoria Cross, his mother, accompanied by a lady friend, came to the Exhibition to see the figure of her son. It was on the 24th of August, 1916.

No sooner did Mrs. Cornwell catch sight of the image of her young hero than she burst into a fit of weeping, and exclaimed, " My boy, my dear boy ! " Upon resuming her composure she expressed her surprise at the remarkable resemblance, and added : " I am very proud of my boy, but I do miss him so."

Mrs. Cornwell had with her a letter she had

U

received from the Captain of H.M.S. *Chester* (her son's ship).   He wrote :

> I know you would wish to hear of the splendid fortitude and courage shown by your boy.   His devotion to duty was an example to all of us.   The wounds, which resulted in his death within a short time, were received in the first few minutes of the action.   He remained steady at his most exposed post at the gun, waiting for orders.   His gun would not bear on the enemy ; all but two of the crew were killed or wounded, and he was the only one who was in such an exposed position.   But he felt he might be needed, as indeed he might have been ; so he stayed there, standing and waiting under heavy fire with just his own brave heart and God's help to support him.

For the model of Captain Fryatt, of the Great Eastern Railway steamer *Brussels*, I had to rely mainly upon photographs.

This brave seaman was captured, with his vessel, by the Germans on the 23rd of June, 1916.   On the 27th of the following month he was condemned to death at Bruges for attempting to ram a German submarine, the sentence being carried out the same afternoon.

The model appropriately stands near that of Mr. Havelock Wilson, the sailors' champion, and, judging from the remarks of visitors who knew the Captain well, it bears a good resemblance.

We cannot leave this subject without associating with these figures the revered names of Lord Roberts and Lord Kitchener, whose models stand near by.   The attitude of visitors towards them is that of deep admiration and respect, expressed not so much by word of mouth as by demeanour, which eloquently testifies to the public sympathy with these great warriors.

Enclosed in a glass case is a walking-stick to which belongs a story showing the kind-heartedness of Queen Alexandra.

Early in the war the Queen-Mother visited the wounded Indian soldiers in hospital at Brighton, and, noticing that one of the officers limped, she inquired of him how he came by his injuries. The officer produced his aluminium ration-box, and explained that a German bullet had struck it, scattering fragments of the metal into his leg and other parts of his body.

Queen Alexandra's sympathy with the Indian officer took a practical form, as she presented him with her own walking-stick to aid him during canvalescence.

Some time afterwards the officer returned to the front, and a brother officer brought the walking-stick to us, as he thought Madame Tussaud's was the best place for it, so that the public should be constantly reminded of Queen Alexandra's deed of kindness.

The stick bears on a silver plate the initial " A.," surmounted by the royal crown.

The incident reminds me of another in connection with the same gracious lady which occurred many

years ago, when the Exhibition was at the old
Portman Rooms in Baker Street.

Queen Alexandra, who was then the Princess of
Wales, had been visiting the Exhibition, and was
leaving the building when a poor flower-girl, with
a baby in her arms, approached her and, before
anyone could intervene, held a small bunch of
violets close to the Princess's face, saying, " Buy
a bunch of violets, please, lady."

Instead of being annoyed, the Princess accepted
the flowers with her usual sweet smile, handed
the girl half-a-sovereign, and then entered her
carriage and drove away.

The astonished girl kept looking at the coin in
her hand, and was quite alarmed when she was
told she had held her flowers under the nose of the
Princess of Wales ; but the remembrance of the
Princess's smile soon reassured her, and she went
away happy.

In the early days of the war the late Duke of
Norfolk, the Duchess, and their two children, the
young Earl of Arundel and his sister, Lady Mary
Howard, formed a quartette of most interested
spectators, and were conducted over the place by
the gentleman who had been appointed as War
Lecturer to the Exhibition.

He devoted most of his attention to the young
people, and relates how the Earl and his sister
passed unobtrusively among the exhibits, gaily

chatting all the way, no one but he recognising the ducal party.

The Earl was shown, and allowed to handle, a German rifle, then recently captured in Belgium, and he instantly pretended to load the weapon. Then, raising it to his shoulder, he took a level aim at the head of the Kaiser and clicked the trigger.

As the party were retiring, his Grace and the Duchess had a brief consultation, after which the Duke came back to thank the lecturer for the attention he had given his son and daughter.

There were sovereigns in those days, and his Grace offered one to the cicerone, who deferentially declined the gift, saying he had been amply rewarded by the pleasure of the young people's company. " I told the Duchess you wouldn't take it," said the Duke, laughing.

CHAPTER XLVII

A crinoline comedy—Mr. Bruce Smith's story—An American
lady's shilling—My father's meeting with Barnum—The
" cherry-coloured cat "—Paganini and the tailor—George
Grossmith poses.

IN the dressing of the models attention must
naturally be paid to the varying styles of both
sexes. For this reason visitors are able to mark
the changes Dame Fashion has decreed.

The crinoline period known to our mothers was,
curiously enough, anticipated in the days
immediately preceding the French Revolution,
as exemplified by the quaint Parisian coquette,
Madame Sappe, with whom that egoistic old cynic,
Voltaire, is palpably flirting in the Grand Hall, a
few paces removed from the portraits of Louis XVI.
and his Queen, Marie Antoinette.

The crinoline of Madame Sappe brings vividly
to mind an amusing story related by my grand-
uncle Joseph, who was standing by the turnstiles
when a portly matron waddled towards the pay-
table, wearing an exaggerated example of this
spacious skirt. Her passage aroused some curiosity,
and the shuffling of her feet was accompanied by

an unaccountable sound of pattering which disposed my relative to keep her under observation.

As soon as she found herself among the figures and hidden from view, as she imagined, the buxom dame cautiously raised her crinoline, when, to my uncle's amazement, out stepped two little boys.

Nothing was said to the adventurous woman who had thus passed her offspring into the Exhibition free, and my uncle used to say that the expression on her face at the success of her subterfuge was one of radiant satisfaction.

Mr. Bruce Smith, the popular artist, who has produced many scenic effects in our tableaux, tells a story perhaps against himself.

He was engaged, with several fellow artists, on a hunting scene, when an elderly lady and a friend strolled quietly past. Mr. Smith, at the moment, was standing stock-still, scanning his work ; then suddenly making a motion with his brush to retouch the canvas, he was startled by an unearthly yell from the old lady :

" Good heavens ! they are alive ! "

Our " Master of the Robes " fell in conversation with an American lady, who told him that she had paid for admission with a shilling given to her in the States by an English aunt with the instruction that if ever she went to London the shilling should be expressly spent on her admission to Madame Tussaud's.

She had related the same story to the money-taker

at the turnstile, and he was so impressed that he laid the romantic shilling on one side. Our representative offered to give it back to the lady, but she thanked him, and said :

"No, I guess I could not break faith with my aunt ! The shilling has found its appointed place in Madame Tussaud's till, after many years, and I have done as I was told."

My father's meeting with Phineas Taylor Barnum, the great showman, was an accidental one.

While lunching in a West End restaurant the brusque and humorous behaviour of one of the guests sitting near enlisted my father's amused attention. The waiters were no less amused by the breezy visitor with the American accent, who supplemented his commands with odd remarks. Having ordered a second dozen of oysters, the American said :

"I guess I could hanker arter these. Bring me another dozen."

Looking hard at him, my father recognised Barnum, and presently the two men were in friendly conversation ; in fact, they spent the greater part of the day together, as kindred spirits are apt to do in such circumstances.

Barnum used to call himself the "Prince of Humbugs," and gave that title to his autobiography. He told my father a story about a bright idea that struck him when his show was going none too well in an American town.

He put up an announcement, " Come and see the cherry-coloured cat," and imposed an extra charge for the privilege.

There was almost a riot as Barnum showed the people a black cat. They protested, and demanded their money back ; but he coolly asked them whether they had never seen a black cherry, and so appeased their wrath.

Barnum sat to me in the spring of 1890, about a year before he died, and I think I must give him the palm for being the most entertaining of all my subjects, his reminiscences extending over so long and interesting a period. I remember him telling me that many years before he had tried to induce my grandfather to transport Madame Tussaud's Exhibition to New York, but that the negotiations fell through at the last moment.

As I modelled him he gave me some gentle hints not to be too attentive to the wrinkles on his face, from which I inferred that the old showman possibly thought he looked older than he felt, in spite of his silvery hair and four-score years.

A short-sighted tailor was once employed to repair the coat worn by Paganini, who stood with the violin under his left arm, while the bow was held aloft in his right hand.

The figure was on a tall pedestal, and the knight of the needle had to use a step-ladder. One of the attendants, ever ready for a joke, taking advantage of the tailor's infirmity, removed the figure, and, adopting a similar attitude, stood in its place.

The tailor prepared his thread, mounted the steps, and was about to begin stitching when the supposed figure brought the bow down on his victim's back. This so terrified the unfortunate man that he rolled down the ladder on to the floor, where he sat gazing up with the utmost stupefaction.

All attempts to pacify him were for a time futile, and whenever he passed the figure of Paganini afterwards he invariably sidled away from it with a scared look.

Another practical joker was the late George Grossmith.

It is on record that he once made the Exhibition the scene of his operations. Getting into an advantageous nook, he stood stock-still in a line with other celebrities—waxen ones. People going by stopped and said:

"Ah, Grossmith! Capital likeness! How excellent! Dear little Grossmith, one would think he was alive!" and various remarks of the kind. Then suddenly the effigy nodded grotesquely, and slowly extended a comic Grossmithian hand. Everyone fled as though he had been shot at.

The Speaker of the House of Commons (Mr. J. W. Lowther), at a banquet given by the Institution of Civil Engineers, in Middle Temple Hall, on the 23rd of March, 1898, told of a distinguished visitor to London who mistook Madame Tussaud's for the House of Commons.

Much the same view must have been taken by a genial and sociable diplomat from the United States who, soon after his arrival in London, came to Madame Tussaud's.

" And what do you think of our great Exhibition ? " asked a friend.

" Well," replied the General, " it struck me as being very like an ord nary English evening party."

CHAPTER XLVIII

As soon as I learned in the winter of 1903 that the
Old Bailey was to be demolished and its mementoes
sold by auction, I hastened to the historic court-
house, armed with a catalogue, to tick off such
articles as might be wanted for Madame Tussaud's.

The grim building brought many impressive
scenes to my recollection, and it struck me as a
curious freak of fate that the place where house-
breakers had been tried and sentenced should now
be itself in the hands of the " house-breakers."

The Royal Arms and the Sword of Justice had
been taken down, and the walls behind the judge's
seat had been stripped of their faded hangings,
giving to the old court an air of desolation ; while
the removal of the doors and windows admitted
the chilly blasts of that bleak February day.

From court to court I passed, noting the cata-
logued items that attracted me. I observed the
long form, covered with black, time-worn leather,
where I sat on the occasion of my first visit, thirty
years before, a sensitive and imaginative youth,

contemplating with awe and a strange depression of spirits the final stages of a murder trial.

Then, as now, it was the interests of Madame Tussaud's that sent me to the Old Bailey, and it may seem odd to confess that of all my many duties none ever afforded me less real pleasure than such duties as this.

This time my visit was unexpectedly relieved by an amusing incident which might have served for a scene in a melodrama.

I came upon a bevy of workmen, in charge of a jovial carpenter, improvising a mock trial to pass the time between the conclusion of a meal and the resumption of their work.

Presently I heard a scuffling noise and the voice of someone in distress. A lanky old man was being forced by a couple of fellow workmen into the prisoners' dock, obviously on some sort of vamped-up charge.

" Silence ! " shouted a shrill-voiced little man, wearing an apron and paper cap, who had made himself usher of the court.

I looked towards the jury-box, and there saw a droll-looking individual finishing his dinner out of a newspaper.

" Stop that row ! Such conduct is disgraceful in a court of justice," he called, looking across at the struggling prisoner.

Then, observing himself to be alone, the occupant of the jury-box managed to empanel six of his

friends to make seven " good men and true."
The jurymen came forward from different sheltered
parts of the court, bringing with them what
remained of their meal.

As by some prearranged signal, an elderly man,
with a round, red face, quietly slipped into the
judge's seat, assuming a judicial air, and fixing
his stern gaze upon the protesting prisoner in the
dock. The judge paid no attention to the banter
directed to him by a number of workmen who
constituted the " public " and had sauntered in
to enjoy the sport.

His " lordship " took on himself the duties of
judge and clerk of the court, and gravely recited
a long and terrible indictment of the accused,
who might have been some arch-fiend from the
list of crimes charged against him—a list that
seemed to box the compass of the Ten Command-
ments. He was involved in domestic complications
which drew forth groans from all in court, and
the judge's reference to his " poor dear wife and
little innocent children " evoked well-simulated
execration.

A comical fellow entered the witness-box, and
reminded the prisoner of a blood-curdling murder
he had committed years ago, for which somebody
else had been hanged. The witness paused, and
then, bringing down his fist, said, " Worse than
all this, my lord, *'e's been known to work overtime
without extra pay.*"

While these harrowing details were visibly moving the jury, the clocks of the neighbourhood struck the close of the dinner hour, and the whole seven men with one accord jumped to their feet shouting " Guilty ! " adding, " No recommendation to mercy."

The judge put on a billycock hat in imitation of the black cap, and addressed the prisoner with due solemnity to this effect :

" Prisoner at the bar, we regret we cannot ask you whether you have anything to say. Justice has no time for that. A jury of your countrymen has found you guilty, and they know best. My duty is to order you to be taken to a public-house near at hand, where you are very well known, and at a certain hour you shall buy drinks for everyone in this court, including myself, the jury, and whatever members of the public care to be present. If you fail to turn up at the appointed time and place, may the Lord have mercy on your stingy soul ! "

In the course of a few days the Old Bailey jury-box and several other fittings of the ancient criminal court were installed under the roof of the Exhibition. The prices they fetched were hardly more than nominal.

It was very different, however, with the relics of the adjoining prison. The mementoes of Old Newgate found many eager buyers, and the bitter February weather did not prevent a large crowd of bidders following the auctioneer about as he crossed the bleak prison yard and passed through the long dreary corridors.

The bidders came from all classes of society, bent on obtaining some keepsake of the sombre establishment. I see that procession now, some muffled to the ears, some blowing their finger-tips in the piercing cold, others stamping their feet, but all indulging in one form of humour or another to keep up their spirits in very dispiriting surroundings.

There were three lots on which the crowd bestowed special attention.

One was Jack Sheppard's cell, from which he made his daring escape—a thrilling feat dear to the imagination of boys young and old.

Another lot was the cell in which Lord George Gordon, the instigator of the riots that bear his name, died of gaol fever on the 1st of November, 1793. His exploits will be remembered by readers of *Barnaby Rudge*.

The third lot was the famous bell which, for just upon a century and a half, had never failed to notify the good citizens of London the precise moment when a condemned prisoner had paid with his life for a life he had taken.

There was an idea at the time that the metal of the Newgate bell contained in it a quantity of silver, and this belief gave rise to the impression that it would fetch a high price.

THE OLD NEWGATE BELL.

Acquired by Madame Tussaud & Sons, Ltd., when the
Prison was demolished in 1903.

[To face p. 305.

But it fell to our bidding, amid a hearty burst of approval, for the round sum of £100, by no means a high price for such a coveted relic.

Not only the bell, but also the cells, came into our possession that day. The thick solid masonry and heavy ironwork were taken down and carefully marked, so that each part should be set up again in its right position when installed at Madame Tussaud's—a tedious process that incurred a far greater outlay than the original cost.

Satisfaction was widely expressed that the Newgate relics should find their way into Tussaud's.

These memorials of Old Newgate have already reposed in their new home sixteen years, and have been viewed by millions of people who otherwise would not have had an opportunity of seeing them.

Visitors of all grades of society linger long before these narrow cells, and I have often seen them rap with their knuckles the Newgate bell, which never fails to respond with a soft mellow resonance, reminding one of the time-honoured couplet, deeply inscribed upon it :

> Ye people all who hear me ring
> Be faithful to your God and King.

W

CHAPTER XLIX

ON very many occasions Madame Tussaud's has been the subject of prose and verse in the public Press. I have already given a few extracts. Here are other quotations, some of which will surely raise a smile.

Tom Hood, the prince of punsters, honoured us with the following quatrain :

> The stillborn figures of Madame Tussaud,
>   With their eyes of glass and their hair of flax,
> They only stare whatever you ax,
>   For their ears, you know, are nothing but wax.

Punch has always been very fond of honouring us with quips and sallies regarding portraits that seemed to merit such good-humoured attention. The dapper and debonair late Poet Laureate, Mr. Alfred Austin, had not long been added to the collection when our genial jester coruscated as follows :

306

ALFRED AMONG THE IMMORTALS.

The Poet Laureate is on View at Madame Tussaud's.

" Let them gibe, let them jeer,
   Let them snigger and sneer
     At my dramas, my lays, and my odes !
   Others know my true worth—
   'Mid the great ones on earth,
     They've enshrined me at Madame Tussaud's."

A more recent contribution from a light versifier runs :

There's a refuge, if Cabinet duties cease,
Where Ministers anxious to rest—with *Peace*—
     May do so.
Political stars who are on the wane
In a popular Chamber may wax again
     Chez Tussaud.

Here is another quotation from *Punch* :

There once was a Madame called Tussaud
Who loved the grand folk in *Who's Who*, so
   That she made them in wax,
   Both their fronts and their backs,
And asked no permission to do so.

One thing is to be noted about the last two quotations : the writer gives the right pronunciation to the name Tussaud, whereas other " poets " often make it rhyme with " swords "—a common error.

There was a picture in *Moonshine*, in which a policeman was separating two quarrelling errand boys.

" Now then, you boys ! " said the officer.

Young Pat : " Shure an' it's all him. Hitting me, an' I've got a uncle a Mimber of Parliament, I have."

Young John : " And what of that ? Why did he cheek me ? I'm as good as him. I've got an uncle in Madame Tussaud's."

The following adroit dialogue appeared in a humorous periodical beneath the picture of a Scottish minister addressing one of two dishevelled youths :

> Minister (to small boy who has been fighting) : " Ah, laddie, think what wad hae bin done tae ye if ye had kilt that laddie ! "
>
> Small Boy : " I'd a bin had up."
>
> Minister : " Ah yes, ye'd a bin had up, but something waur than that."
>
> Small Boy : " I'd a bin hang, mebbie."
>
> Minister : " Yes ! but something waur than that wad a happen'd."
>
> Small Boy : " After that I'd a bin pit in Madame Tussaud's."

The family name often appears in the public Press without much rhyme or reason. The following verse published at the time of the Hague Peace Conference in 1899 is somewhat apropos at the present moment :

> When all are agreed in word and deed
>   That pacific intentions shall rule,
> When armies disband on every hand
>   And tin soldiers are not used at school,
> When rifles and swords are shown at Tussaud's
>   As inventions quite obsolete,
> Then we might be pleasant, but just at present
>   We're thinking 'bout keeping our Fleet.

When the portrait model of Mr. Rudyard Kipling was added to the Exhibition, that gentleman was made the subject of the following lines :

What though from distant climes
  I, young, unknown,
Swift from obscurity
  Sprang to a throne?

What though aforetime
  Worship was paid me?
Though offers fabulous
  Publishers made me?

What though the critics all
  Pleasantly flattered me?
What though all this befell
  (As if *this* mattered) me?

Now with sublime head
  Strike I the stars;
Better is this to me
  Than all their " pars."

Modelled in wax at last,
  Now they do show me
With other famous ones,
  Madame Tussaud me!

Now may I pose supreme!
  Now to me, *à la*
" Crowned heads," the public grant
  Their great Valhalla!

Now may the universe
  Echo my name;
Now nothing more remains,
  This—this is FAME!

CHAPTER L

IF I have recounted many stories relating to incidents that have taken place long after Madame Tussaud passed away, it is because the flow of anecdote prompted by her genius has continued in an unbroken course down to the present times.

But the atmosphere of romance that pervades this history belongs in the main to her days, and it is only fitting that with the close of her days it should practically come to an end.

She died some eight years before I was born, but from my father and from those of his generation who spent the best part of their lives in her company I learnt so much about her that it is difficult for me to realise that I had not enjoyed her personal acquaintance. Her model that stands at the head of the "Sleeping Beauty," I have always been given to understand, is a speaking likeness.

In figure she was small and slight, and her manner was vivacious. Her complexion was fresh, her hair dark brown with never more than a sprinkling of grey, and her soft brown eyes were keen and

310

FRANCIS TUSSAUD.
Younger son of Madame Tussaud.
Born, 1800 ; died, 1873.

(*Modelled by his son Joseph, and exhibited at the Royal Academy*)

[To face p. 311

alert when her interest was aroused. She was a great talker, her conversation was replete with reminiscences, and, moreover, she was blessed with a faultless memory. Austere in her habits of life, exacting in her likes and dislikes, she showed a ready sympathy with those in distress, and, above all, she was generous to a fault.

Unfortunately her *Memoirs*, published in 1838, although they were penned more than a decade before she died, do not bring us into any very close relationship with either her personality or her life.

This would not be surprising to those who knew her, or who were acquainted with the circumstances in which they were written. She seldom could be brought to speak of herself and her own painful experiences ; and at no time did she betray the slightest disposition to thrust herself upon the public. She was seventy-eight years old at the time, and her desire for seclusion grew stronger as years advanced, until her entourage became narrowed down to the simple companionship of her immediate family circle.

The *Memoirs* came to be written in this wise :

Her two sons, Joseph and Francis, in collaboration with an old literary friend of the name of Francis Hervé, settled in their minds that the old lady should be induced to leave behind her an account of her career.

As she had declared her unwillingness to busy

herself with the task of compiling her autobiography
—and in certain matters we know her to have been
immovable—they decided that the best way of
accomplishing their design would be to record the
substance of those conversations in which they
rightly surmised they would have little difficulty
in inducing her to take part when in the humour.

In spite of the facilities these gentlemen had
for obtaining the matter used in their publication,
it may be well conjectured that they did not always
find their course run smooth, and at times they
must have been put to odd shifts and a good deal
of careful strategy when gathering what they
wanted from the shrewd old lady without arousing
her suspicions.

For these reasons the *Memoirs* have failed to supply
what is best worth knowing, such as details giving
an insight to her own life—an omission which,
I fear, can never now be made entirely good.
That work is, therefore, made up of disjointed,
scrappy matter, avowedly well written, but somehow obviously strung together for the making
of a book.

In perusing its pages the reader thus finds himself
confronted by a mere procession of notables whom
the old lady happened to have known or to have
seen in her day, each with an encyclopædic quantum
of information tagged to his or her name that might
well have been culled from any biographical
treasury. So it is she is to be found speaking of

others when her reader's one desire is that she should be induced to talk of herself.

Neither does this "Romance" claim to be a biography. Such an undertaking would demand of us closer and more careful study than these brief sketches have entailed, and much diligent research. Moreover, such has not been the purpose of these pages.

By those who had the best authority to speak of her I have been often reminded of the trials and hardships against which she had to battle during her long and strenuous career, showing a courage and determination that might well have broken the spirit of many a man. In estimating her character and her achievements, my mind turns to events of the past few years which have demonstrated how capable women are of enacting a great part in the drama of human life.

Madame Tussaud brought cheerfulness and geniality to bear upon the tasks that lay before her, and therein lay the secret of her triumphs. She was diligent and attentive to her business, devoted to her family, and attached to her friends.

The measure of her years far exceeded the allotted span, and she was rewarded, despite the slightness of her frame, with an almost unbroken continuation of good health, until, on the 15th of April, 1850, she passed peacefully and painlessly away at her house attached to the Exhibition in Baker Street.

Forty years of her life had been chiefly spent

in Paris, and the latter fifty years mostly in London ;
so that her biography may be said to comprise a
tale of two cities.   She was buried in the catacombs
of St. Mary's Church, Cadogan Place, Chelsea.

The last words she spoke in this world were
characteristic of this wonderful woman's indomitable
spirit. Calling her sons, Joseph and Francis, to
her bedside, she gently upbraided them for showing
distress at her departure, rather than gratitude
that she had been spared to them so long.   Her
farewell exhortation was, " I divide my property
equally between you, and implore you, above
all things, never to quarrel."

INDEX

Odhams, Ltd., 39 King Street, London, W.C. 2.